**etiquette
for the businessman**
at home and abroad

By the same author

etiquette
for the businessman

at home and abroad

mary bosticco

Illustrated by michael ffolkes

London

BUSINESS PUBLICATIONS LIMITED

First published 1967

A BUSINESS MANAGEMENT BOOK

This book has been set in 11 on 12 pt Georgian by Richard Clay (The Chaucer Press), Limited, Bungay, Suffolk, for the publishers Business Publications Limited (registered office: 180 Fleet Street, London, E.C.4), publishing offices: Mercury House, Waterloo Road, London, S.E.1

MADE AND PRINTED IN GREAT BRITAIN

TO MY MOTHER

Contents

Acknowledgments

A number of people have helped me with my research for this book. I am very grateful to them all and take this opportunity publicly to thank them.

Peter Townend was a most reliable, enthusiastic, and cheerful guide in all matters pertaining to forms of address and precedence. Dr T. L. V. Blair was most illuminating on the subject of Africa and W. H. Solf was no less so on Japan. Moss Bros. Limited were extremely helpful on all matters concerned with correct attire, while Frank Smythson Limited of New Bond Street were a mine of information with regard to visiting cards, invitations, and so on.

I am most grateful to the 3-M Company for permission to quote their list of 'Ten Most Unwanted Meeting Birds' and to Dr George Copeman for permitting me to quote from his book, *Laws of Business Management and the Executive Way of Life.**

My sincere thanks to the Islamic Cultural Centre for their courteous help, to Max Baumann for his invaluable help in deciphering a mighty German tome, and a very special 'Thank you' to the whole staff of Slough Central Library and to the Librarian of Wycombe College of Art and Technology. Every single one of them went way beyond the call of duty to be of help to me and, indeed, without them, my task would have been ten times greater.

Many thanks also to Olwen Francis, Margaret Gärtner, Lady Cecilia Howard, Rosamind Julius, Beverley Hilton, and Audrey

* Second Edition, Business Publications Limited, 1963.

Slaughter. Also to my cousin, Alessandro Fornier, to Brian Haynes, Thomas J. Evans, Ronald A. Mills, Dominic Roberts, and P. R. Zimmerman.

Bourne End, April, 1967   MB

chapter one

introduction

Good manners are an inestimable asset to the businessman. They help him to win and keep customers and they promote goodwill for himself and his company. Good manners make the daily conduct of business smoother and pleasanter both for the businessman's own staff and for all with whom he comes in contact.

A knowledge of etiquette is a short cut to success for the ambitious young executive. It will give him poise and assurance and prepare him to seize his opportunities as they come along, secure in the knowledge that he knows how to behave in any situation. Not only will he feel at ease with all kinds of people at every educational level and of every cultural and ethnic background, but he will be able to put others at ease. He will be master of every situation.

An executive greeting a customer in his shirtsleeves, talking with a cigar in his mouth or allowing a door to slam in someone's face impresses everyone not so much with his sheer bad manners, but with his poor business judgment, for bad manners are never good business. His boorishness, as the formidable Emily Post has so aptly pointed out,* casts doubts upon his ability and his

* *Emily Post's Etiquette.* Revised by Elizabeth L. Post, Funk & Wagnells, Inc., New York, Eleventh Edition, 1965.

awkwardness irritates and embarrasses. His ignorance stands naked before all. Yet he may believe that good manners belong in 'society' and have no place in the life of a tough, hard-hitting businessman such as himself. Hence his poor judgment, of course. He does not realize that thoughtfulness and regard for the rights and feelings of others are fundamental to both social and business life. If anything, we have more opportunities in business of practising our social skills.

But what is etiquette and what are good manners? Etiquette is a set of agreed conventions governing our relations with others, while the essence of good manners is thoughtfulness and consideration for others. Good manners always take precedence over etiquette and thoughtful people never hesitate to break a rule of etiquette to save someone from embarrassment.

Since mere etiquette is valueless without good manners, it is perhaps best to think of etiquette as being composed of two parts: good manners plus a set of agreed conventions.

Good manners are the essential and immutable part of etiquette. They are the same the world over and a thoughtful, considerate person could travel far without offending anyone, even if ignorant of the accepted conventions, which vary from country to country and from generation to generation.

It is good manners rather than etiquette which cause you to put a stranger at ease in your home; it is good manners which enable you to travel to distant countries without causing offence with your different customs. If, in addition to good manners, you master the accepted conventions of behaviour not only at home, but especially when you travel abroad, you will stand out as a man of polish to the benefit both of yourself and your company.

No doubt there are some conventions which will seem to you quite unimportant and there is no reason why an executive – secure at the pinnacle of his career – should not cheerfully ignore them, just like 'Lord So-and-So' who, according to Gracie Fields, advised her: 'If you feel like putting bread in your soup, put the blasted bread in.'

Whether it would be wise for a young and ambitious executive to follow 'Lord So-and-So's' advice is quite another matter. Unquestionably, he would do far better to refrain from eating his peas with a knife until such time as he is safely on his company's

Board of Directors, but by then, of course, he will have become so accustomed to following all the trivial conventions that he will have not the slightest urge to put bread in his soup or to brandish a chop in his fingers.

chapter two

the executive look

It is extremely important for the business executive always to be well-dressed and well-groomed. A well-cut suit and a cared-for appearance give a man more confidence than any other single thing. Whether he is about to address a large gathering, tackle an irate customer or attend a Board meeting, the knowledge that he is well turned-out will free his mind to solve the immediate problem and add immeasurably to his self-assurance.

For the junior executive on his way up, a neat, well-groomed appearance, free from eccentricities, will do very much more for him than a Beatle haircut.

Fortunately, this does not mean that every businessman in the realm should dress in the same way. Britain is still a land of individuals – for the time being at least – and the businessman has a great deal of latitude in selecting his wardrobe. In fact, one cannot rightly speak of an 'executive look'. There are two, or perhaps even three, quite legitimate executive looks in Britain:

1 First of all there is the world-renowned 'City gent' look: striped trousers, black coat, bowler hat, and rolled umbrella. If you yourself are a traditional City man, then quite ob-

viously you will know exactly how to dress and will need the help of no one.

2 Secondly there is the 'creative executive', for want of a better term. He is usually an art director with an advertising agency or the editor of a quality magazine. He is usually a man of taste and individuality and permits himself to deviate as much as he pleases from the traditional. He gets away with it because the creative person is supposed to be unconventional. This is why copywriters, artists, and designers on the way up can get away with long hair, baggy trousers, and a general air of neglect and *insouciance*. They are, in fact, the same people who, upon reaching the top of their career ladder, blossom out into elegant gentlemen with red linings to their jackets, a carnation buttonhole and collarless coats.

3 The third kind of executive look is the one which we are concerned with here. It is conservative without being dull. It follows the general trend of male fashion, but is not its standard-bearer.

This executive look will consist of a well-cut lounge suit, perhaps in one of the new lighter-weight cloths. It will be either dark blue, with or without a pin stripe, or grey. It will be worn either with a matching waistcoat or without, and a white or striped shirt will go with it.

A conservative tie is best. It could well be a maroon tie with matching socks with a grey suit and, of course, neither an old school tie nor a club tie is out of place.

Socks should stay up, not concertina down to the ankles and there are several types on the market to fill the bill. The shortie socks, while extremely attractive, are best left to after-business hours.

With a blue or grey suit, shoes should be black, and fortunately there are no taboos, even suede shoes being acceptable nowadays.

As for the breast-pocket handkerchief, fashions change as to whether it should show a straight edge, two points, one point, or be tucked in with apparent nonchalance.

If you feel the need to pinion your tie, the tie-tack is the latest way to do it. Tie bars are on their way out and considered undesirable in some quarters.

Most 'authorities' frown on the wearing of pens and pencils in breast pockets. However, for practical reasons, some well-turned-out businessmen solve this problem by having the waistcoat and jacket breast pockets cut deeply enough to conceal pens and pencils completely.

Many people of both sexes strenuously object to the wearing of braces, but men who like wearing them naturally enough put up a very energetic defence. Certainly it is a harmless enough habit, if a trifle old-fashioned. The important thing is – keep your little secret to yourself. If you like wearing braces, by all means do so, but if you take off your jacket at the office, then remove your braces also, just as you would remove your waistcoat in similar circumstances. It is only fair to admit that the sight of a pair of braces, however gay, smacks of the bedroom, not the board room, and is best avoided.

So much then for your everyday wear. For formal occasions, as indicated in Chapter 6, you will need to wear either evening dress or morning dress, as detailed below:

Evening dress: Single-breasted dinner-jacket with either a shawl or step collar, soft white shirt, either pleated or plain, black bow-tie with pointed or straight ends, cummerbund to match the tie, black trousers with a single row of braid, black patent leather shoes without toecaps, black silk or nylon socks.

The cummerbund does not have to be black, but it should match the tie. Some men select a maroon cummerbund and tie. The coloured dinner-jacket is also finally catching on in Britain. It can be maroon, Madras cotton plaid, midnight blue and, of course, white for summer wear.

Tails are worn with a white stiff shirt with white wing collar, white bow tie, white waistcoat, black trousers with a double row of braid, black patent leather shoes without toecaps, black silk or nylon socks. Gloves are no longer worn with evening dress, except at Old Time dances. The edge of the waistcoat should be level with the sides of the coat, not show underneath.

Morning dress: This consists of a black or grey cut-away jacket, soft white shirt with a starched linen collar, striped or grey trousers, black shoes with plain toecaps, black socks.

Three kinds of tie can be worn with the morning suit: the

ordinary tie, which for a festive occasion can be either grey silk or black with a quiet pattern, and for a funeral should be black; the bow tie and the stock. The last two in grey sink are suitable for festive occasions.

For a funeral or memorial service, waistcoat, tie, gloves, and top hat should be black. For festive occasions, the waistcoat and gloves can be grey, buff or patterned – a grey top-hat is usually worn in preference to black and spongebags can be worn instead of striped trousers.

At weddings, younger men seldom bother with gloves and hats, since they are only worn for a few minutes before entering the church.

Tails and morning dress are mostly hired nowadays. This enables you to wear the most up-to-date version on every important occasion and saves you the trouble and expense of buying clothes and accessories which you seldom have occasion to wear.

Dressing on a budget

The young executive on the way up sometimes has difficulty in achieving the standard of appearance he aims for because his salary does not yet allow him sufficient margin.

Such a young man would do well to bear in mind that his money is best invested in a good hand-tailored suit, for a well-cut, hand-tailored suit will outlast and surpass two ordinary suits. This does not mean that our young man will have to cut down on food and patronize one of the leading tailors. If he lives in or near London, he should do a little scouting around to find himself one of those excellent but obscure tailors who ply their trade in the suburbs. He should seek out the small shop with a tailor in the back room actually working on a suit. Let him not be deterred by the flashy models in the windows. They are there to attract the local High Street trade. It does not mean that the tailor cannot make a perfectly conservative suit in the best hand-tailoring tradition. Such tailors usually have a stock of excellent materials to choose from and are only too pleased to make a suit to their customer's personal requirements.

If our young man is not too sure of what he really ought to

B

have as an aspiring top executive, he can buy himself a copy of *Tailor & Cutter* and ask his tailor to copy one of the suits illustrated.

Our young executive on a budget would certainly do well to order two pairs of trousers with his suit, as this will lengthen the life of the outfit. If he chooses a dark grey flannel suit, he will be able to wear the trousers with a sports jacket for leisure wear. Later on, when he adds another suit to his wardrobe, he would do well to stick to the same colour-scheme so that he can wear all his ties and socks with each suit.

If it is to be one overcoat only for all occasions, it should be chosen with great care, so that it is neither too tweedy, nor too dressy. Perhaps a dark shortie coat might be the answer.

All businessmen, whether up-and-coming or at the top of the ladder, should wear a hat. A hat confers dignity and inspires confidence – and a businessman needs both.

Clothes care

If you take good care of your clothes you will prolong their life, and make sure you are always impeccably groomed. A suit should be brushed and hung up on a properly-shaped hanger every time it is taken off. If at all possible, the same suit should never be worn two days running, since a rest is just as good for a suit as for a person. While resting, a suit sheds its wrinkles and its fibres regain their former resilience.

If you use a trouser-press, make sure it is the right kind, as some of them only emphasize any bagging there may be at the knees.

One of Britain's leading men's outfitters recommends brushing a suit every night, pressing it every week and having it dry-cleaned every three months. This sounds like an admirable rule of thumb, but an important point to bear in mind is how often the suit has been worn and what it is made of. For instance, a worsted will keep its shape longer than a non-twist cloth, while the new light-weight cloths crease rather more easily.

Most good men's outfitters have pressing and repairing services and a great number of well-dressed men do their own trouser pressing. Some of them operate on the floor, away from the constraint of ironing board or table.

'. . . you will prolong their life'

Care of self

It should hardly be necessary to add that the well-groomed executive takes as good care of his person as of his clothes and is never in such a hurry as to forego his daily bath or shower, or omit to attend to his teeth, his finger-nails and his hair.

Since it is so easy to forget to have a haircut until reminded by secretary or wife, some impeccably-groomed men have a standing appointment with their barber once a week. In this way, their hair always looks immaculate and never shows the least signs of needing attention.

There are innumerable pleasant toiletries for men on the market now and it is definitely not effeminate to use them. In fact, it is downright offensive not to make regular use of some of them.

chapter three

good manners at
the office

The well-mannered executive is courteous to all – customers and suppliers, superiors, colleagues, and subordinates. Whether a caller is a salesman or one of his own best customers, he tries not to keep him waiting unnecessarily. When he is expecting a visitor, he advises the receptionist ahead of time and makes sure there will be a chair in his office to accommodate him. If he is expecting a number of people, he makes arrangements before-hand to have additional chairs brought in.

If he has been working in his shirt-sleeves, the well-mannered executive puts on his jacket as soon as a visitor is announced. He always rises to greet a woman caller, and usually does so for a man. When he rises to greet a man, they usually shake hands, but this is not necessary if the caller is a woman, unless, of course, she offers her hand.

Since a visitor is not supposed to sit down until invited to do so, it is courteous to offer a seat without delay and to remain standing until the visitor is seated.

Once your visitor is seated, courtesy demands that you give

him your undivided attention. Do not expect him to talk to you while you shuffle papers, sign your mail or turn your back on him. You should sit and listen and look at your visitor while he speaks. If you habitually have constant telephone calls, you can arrange for your secretary to take them.

But if you *are* taking phone calls, finish your sentence or let your visitor finish his, say: 'Will you excuse me, please?' and then pick up your receiver.

The truly courteous executive makes his visitor feel like a v.i.p. by appearing to have all the time in the world to listen to him. If necessary, he makes arrangements for his secretary to interrupt him at a prearranged time and if the visitor does not take the hint, he then finally says: 'I'm afraid I'm due at a meeting.'

A man always stands up when his visitor rises to leave. If his visitor is a woman, he accompanies her at least as far as the door of his office and opens it for her. If the visitor is a man, he may or may not shake hands with him on leaving and sometimes sees him as far as the door. If the way out is in any way difficult to find, it is courteous to see your visitor as far as the lift or the top of the stairs.

When making company policies it is an excellent plan to examine them also from the point of view of good manners, for an aggressive sales policy will only defeat its own purpose if it is also discourteous to prospective customers. One such policy which the general public strongly objects to is the practice of sending out a salesman, unheralded and unannounced, in response to a written inquiry. This is extremely discourteous, assuming as it does that the 'prospect's' time is of no consequence and that he should make himself available to the salesman whenever he may appear.

This practice, which combines bad manners with bad business, is unfortunately spreading, yet its net result is an antagonized customer, plus loss of time and money through fruitless journeys. How much more fruitful to make an appointment ahead of time.

Dealing with superiors

Your superior, whether he be the company chairman, the managing director or indeed a department head if you are a junior executive, has a right to expect from you the same common courtesy, thoughtfulness, and respect which you would grant to any person of greater age or experience. And this, of course, applies even if your chief happens to be a younger man than you are, as so frequently happens nowadays.

Companies vary tremendously in their degrees of formality or informality and in their atmosphere, and it is up to the executive who joins a company to fit in with the situation he finds. If you happen to dislike intensely a very formal atmosphere, then you must not join a very formal company, for it is not up to you to change a company's atmosphere, but rather to adapt yourself to it. If, on the other hand, you have been used to a very old-fashioned, formal, and stuffy atmosphere and move to a breezy, informal office you would do well to suit your manner to it. The well-mannered man 'fits in', he does not insist on swimming against the tide.

The same applies in dealing with your chief himself. At first your sensitive antennae will be drawn out full length and you will quickly learn to avoid those things which irritate him and to adapt yourself to his way of working. This does not mean that you should become a 'yes-man' or a sycophant. Such men are absolutely useless to a top executive, who needs men with opinions of their own and the courage to stick to them. It simply means that you would do well to study his likes and dislikes and avoid ruffling his feathers, if only in your own interest.

Not all top executives abhor the same things, but here are some of the things some of them dislike:

1 UNPUNCTUALITY Even if the top executive is sometimes late for a meeting he likes his subordinates to be punctual.

2 LACK OF FLEXIBILITY A top executive likes to feel that his staff are willing to adapt their working day and sometimes even their private life to his requirements.

3 WOOLLY THINKERS A top executive heartily dislikes a man who conceals his thoughts in a morass of verbiage and reservations with the result that perfectly valid points do not come to light until the meeting is over.

4 WINDBAGS A top executive does not like a man who beats

about the bush for ten minutes before he gets to the point, nor a man who constantly sends him verbose reports.

5 DISORGANIZATION A top executive does not like having a meeting with someone who is constantly shuffling his papers looking for documents which should have been put in the right order beforehand.

6 THE BUCK-PASSER Having delegated certain responsibilities to one of his staff, the top executive expects him to get on with the job and make his own decisions. The insecure executive who constantly needs his decisions confirmed from on high is not going to endear himself to his chief.

7 OVER-FAMILIARITY The top executive takes a dim view of the man who presumes on a familiarity which does not exist, particularly if this is done to impress a colleague with how close he is to the chairman.

8 A POOR SENSE OF PRIORITIES Nothing infuriates a man more than to see a subordinate getting his priorities hopelessly muddled. This applies more to the department head, since a managing director and a chairman expect *their* subordinates to get on with the job in their own way.

9 SELF-CENTREDNESS A top executive likes a man who is aware of the other person's problems as well as his own. In other words, an executive should strive to see his chief's point of view, as well as his own.

Very few of the nine points mentioned are, strictly speaking, concerned with good manners. Many of them have to do with efficiency and you will find that many of the things which irritate colleagues and even subordinates are due to lack of efficiency rather than downright bad manners. Thus, the achievement of a harmonious working relationship with superiors, colleagues, and subordinates calls for a combination of efficiency, thoughtfulness, and courtesy – quite a tall order for most of us.

Dealing with colleagues

While you may only see your chief briefly once or twice a week, you will probably be in daily contact with at least some of your colleagues and will certainly be working closely with one or more of them. It is therefore essential that your relations be as smooth and harmonious as possible.

Nothing can help more to achieve this end than courtesy and consideration at all times. The first thing a colleague whose department works closely with yours will expect of you is co-operation. He will expect you to send him carbons of letters and memoranda which concern his department and generally to keep him posted on matters that concern him.

Should you need to consult him, do not attempt to summon him to your office as if he were a subordinate, but go and see *him*. Neither should you descend on him without warning and expect him to lay aside his work and give you an hour or more of his time. If your visit is likely to be prolonged, it is more considerate to phone and ask him or his secretary whether he is free to see you. Apart from being the more courteous approach, it will save you an unnecessary trip to his office, should he have visitors or be out. Do not enter a colleague's office – or anyone's office – smoking. To do so and then to stub out your cigarette in his ashtray is very rude indeed. If he happens to be a non-smoker, it is quite unpardonable.

If your colleague has a problem to discuss with you, then it is up to him to come to your office. In other words, colleagues usually alternate visits to each other's offices, although all kinds of variations to the theme can be made to suit particular conditions. If one has a quieter office, for instance, it will be favoured for some meetings. If another has a larger office, then, obviously a meeting involving several people would more sensibly take place there.

It should be emphasized, however, that there are no hard and fast rules on the subject and nothing could be more petty than to add up the score to find out whose turn it is to go to whose office. It is always best to show the other man that you are 'bigger' than he is, rather than be equally small and force him to come to you.

Needless to say, when a colleague comes to your office, you should give him the same undivided attention you pay to other visitors. Giving him one ear while you continue with your work is not good enough.

At times, you may want to enlist the help of a colleague's

subordinates in a project of your own. It is courteous in such cases to approach your colleague, rather than go direct to his subordinates. Frequently, of course, such an arrangement is made in the course of a meeting to discuss the project with a colleague, and in this case it is perfectly in order to approach his subordinates direct, since he will no doubt already have told them about the work.

Providing you bear in mind the principle that a colleague's subordinates should be approached through him and with his approval, a number of variations to suit the circumstances can then be used.

In dealing with your colleagues, your guiding lights should be courtesy, thoughtfulness, and tact, not only for their sake, but also in your own interest, for this is the best way to gain their co-operation and respect.

Dealing with subordinates

The true measure of a man is gauged by his treatment of his subordinates. The petty man will bow and scrape to his superiors, while venting his spite and bad manners on his subordinates, who cannot hit back.

Fortunately, courteous treatment results in greater co-operation on the part of its recipient, so that good manners and self-interest are allied. This means that, even with subordinates, it *pays* to be well-mannered.

Everyone likes a boss who is cheerful, friendly and polite. They like to be greeted with a friendly 'Good morning' or, if they beat you to it, they like to get a reply, not a grunt. They like a boss who says 'Thank you' and 'Please'. They like him to use such expressions as: 'Would you mind doing so-and-so?', 'I suggest you tackle it this way', or, 'This one is rather urgent, I'm afraid.'

The days of order-giving are over and it is, in fact, just as easy to ask for something to be done as it is to issue commands. The only difference is that the polite request is far more likely to be efficacious these days.

Thoughtfulness is another trait which everyone likes to find in a boss. If you are the owner of a small business it is natural enough to want to go on working well into the evening, but it is thoughtful to realize that your men, however much they may enjoy their job, are anxious to get home to their wives and families at 'knocking off' time. Likewise, a subordinate executive may have a luncheon engagement and it is thoughtful to inquire, rather than to go rambling on without consideration for him. Some top executives seem to have no need for a midday snack, but they should not assume the same in others.

Thoughtlessness, or lack of consideration, is perhaps the most universal failing of a man towards his subordinates. He does not recognize that they have a life outside of business. He may have a one-track mind – nothing counts for him but business – and he thinks that all his employees should be the same. He loses sight of two things: one, that if he has a one-track mind, it is his failing not his virtue; and two, his subordinates are not usually getting as much out of it as he is.

As for reprimanding or criticizing a subordinate, good manners demand that you do this in private. Good management practice, however, demands that you do it not at all. It is a complete fallacy to maintain that fault-finding is not only permissible, but necessary in the superior/subordinate relationship. Criticism has a completely negative effect on a man. It simply forces him to defend himself and turn his own criticism upon his superior. Nothing does more to kill a man's ambition than criticism from his superior.

This simple fact has been realized and acted upon like a burning tenet of faith by some of the most successful executives the world has ever known, very much including Charles Schwab, one of the only two men in history to be paid a salary of a million dollars a year. Charles Schwab considered his greatest asset to be his ability to get the best out of people. 'I never criticize anyone,' he maintained.

So once again, good manners and good management go hand in hand.

It is extremely rude to take advantage of the fact that a man works for you by getting him to do all manner of extra-curricular tasks for you and to put his personal talent or reputation at your disposal. Quite a number of employers make a habit of getting their employees to do everything from sketching to gardening for them personally, without its ever occurring to them that this is an imposition, as well as being highly reprehensible.

Your secretary and you

Innumerable books have been written on how to be a perfect
secretary yet, strangely enough, little seems to have been written
on how to be a passing fair boss. With the increasingly tight
market in secretaries, it is perhaps time that the employer
examined his own behaviour to see how he measures up.

Your secretary is your closest subordinate and consequently it
is she who suffers most if you are not courteous and considerate.
Apart from the points already mentioned, there are others which
apply more specifically to your secretary.

Some men seem to think we are still living in the Middle Ages
and treat their secretary like a personal servant. 'Pull that blind
down,' 'Take this tray out,' and so on. This sort of behaviour is
extremely rude and quite uncalled for. A secretary is not a personal valet, even though she may take on a few mothering and
nursing chores of her own free will.

Secretaries like a well-organized man who collects his dictation
together, calls her in at a regular time every day, perhaps first
thing in the morning before the interruptions begin, and gets on
with it until it is finished. Nothing irritates a secretary more than
to be called in every hour to be given one four-line memorandum.

It is equally irritating to be given a large batch of urgent letters
at the end of the day.

In fact, the great majority of a secretary's grievances are connected in one way or the other with dictation. Here are some of
the things your secretary does not like:

1 The man who puffs cigar smoke all over her or hisses his
letters at her through his pipe. If he adds insult to injury by
placing his cigarette-butts right under her nose, she puts him
down as a very rude man indeed.

2 The man who paces the floor like a caged lion while dictating
his letters. Perhaps pacing the floor inspires him, but it is
most inconsiderate of him to expect his secretary to catch his
words from the back of his neck, as it were.

3 The man who keeps her sitting for hours beside his desk
while he makes a phone call he has suddenly thought of.

Her time may not be as valuable as his, but it does have *some* value, none the less, and she would be far happier getting on with the filing rather than wasting time awaiting his pleasure.

4 The man who speaks indistinctly and does not have his thoughts organized.

5 The man whose English is abominable, yet who resents his secretary's improvements to his letters.

A secretary sometimes has occasion to go out on business with her chief and she may have lunch with him, or even dinner once in a great while when business circumstances warrant it. She will certainly be trained to do the right thing on such occasions and it is no less up to her chief to show her the same consideration as he would to any other woman.

If you know you may have to take your secretary with you on occasional business trips, you will want to make sure you employ one who is at least 21, and preferably a few years older. Travelling with a secretary can be a situation of some delicacy and it is up to you as a gentleman and her superior to make quite sure that nothing you do or say during the whole of the trip could possibly be misconstrued by anyone.

However poised and experienced a girl may be, she is bound to be slightly apprehensive at the prospect of being away from home with you for the first time and it is up to you to put her at ease.

You will want to make sure that rooms are reserved on separate floors. Some people even go as far as staying at separate hotels, but there is really no need to go so far. You will meet in the dining-room for breakfast or elsewhere as convenient, but you will never, on any account, go banging on her door.

There is no reason why she should not join you socially in the evening, when convenient, as you certainly would not want her to spend every evening alone in a strange town.

Meetings

Good manners and consideration for others are essential to every kind of meeting if it is to be a success. If you are leading the meeting you will certainly draw up an agenda ahead of time and send copies to all participants so that they may brief themselves and collect together the material they wish to present at the meeting.

It will be up to you to keep the meeting moving, to encourage everyone to take part, and prevent any one person from dominating the proceedings. If participants have a lot to say, they will sometimes all start speaking at once, and it is up to the chairman to keep proceedings under control. You can look directly at one of the speakers, in the hope that the others will let him have his say. If they all persist in talking together, you can break in with: 'What was that, Bill? I couldn't quite hear.' This should certainly quieten the others. When you have heard Bill out, you should be sure to turn to those who were speaking before and say something like: 'I believe you had a comment to make on this, Jim?'

Before closing the meeting, the conclusions reached should be neatly summed up and who is to do what clearly spelled out. So many meetings end inconclusively with everyone assuming that someone else is going to take care of the things mentioned.

If you are not leading a meeting but participating, you can help your chairman immensely by your courtesy and consideration. You will arrive at the meeting prepared, having thought about the subject and brought with you any relevant material. You will take your turn to bat, as it were, letting the other fellow have his say, too. You will address your remarks to the chairman, not go into a huddle with your next-door neighbour and air your views privately to him. If your neighbour should try this on you, you will discourage him with a non-committal remark. You will not seize the opportunity to air your own small grievances or to ride your particular hobby-horse.

Above all, you will *participate* in the discussion, not merely occupy a chair. The meeting was called in order to hear everyone's views and it is up to you to contribute to it. So important is this point that the 3M Company, which is reputed to be one of the best-managed corporations in the u.s.a., recently drew up a list of the 'Ten Most Unwanted Meeting Birds' and almost every one of these nefarious creatures turned out to be a non-participator. It should be noted that in American English a bird is a feathered biped, no more and no less. Here are those obnoxious 'Meeting Birds':

1 GRAND CANYON YAWNER A very inactive meeting bird, the Grand Canyon Yawner has never missed a company meeting. He spends endless hours in today's meeting happily contemplating tomorrow's meeting.

Sundry Meeting Birds

2 SLEEPY-HEADED ELBOW LEANER A nocturnal meeting bird, he's the master of the art of sleeping with his eyes open. The open coat allows him to sleep without snoring.

3 THE WHITE PIPE CLEANER Finds the meeting room an excellent perch for catching up on chores the wife-bird forbids at

home. The meeting room is his favourite habitat for testing the fragrance of an old pipe or lusty cigar.

4 THE DARK-SUITED MAGAZINE READER The wisest of the Meeting Birds, the Magazine Reader instinctively 'tunes out' any meeting presentation.

5 THE LEFT-HANDED DOODLER Loves to listen to others, nod his head and shuffle papers. Avoids bad decisions by making no decisions.

6 THE CROSS-LEGGED FINGER-NAIL CHECKER This species finds the meeting the perfect climate for preening feathers and planning vacations.

7 THE FIDGETY TIME-CHECKER Resents time-wasting meetings which deter him from such important corporate functions as lunch or market surveys of secretarial dating problems.

8 THE CIGAR-CHEWING MANAGER BIRD Easily identified by a nervous twitch, a strong tendency to rule the roost, and the absence of a listening mechanism.

9 THE GLASSY-EYED DREAMER Finds meetings very useful for dreaming up methods of rescuing maidens trapped by evil old magicians.

10 THE SUGAR-TONGUED LOVE BIRDS Found only in pairs. Usually inhabit engineering, legal, or accounting departments. Marked by rapid speech, high technical data, and a strong mutual survival instinct.

Giving and receiving gifts

Many companies have a policy which forbids its executives to accept costly gifts from suppliers and prospective suppliers. If your company has such a policy, obviously, you will follow it. Certainly it is not in good taste to offer an expensive gift to someone whom you wish to influence in any way. Neither is it in good taste to give very personal gifts to women subordinates, or, indeed, to women in general.

If you want to show your appreciation to your women subordinates with a gift at Christmas, choose perfume or toiletries, chocolates, a book token or other gift token. Wearing apparel is not suitable, with the possible exception of silk scarves, which are always very acceptable and not too intimate a gift. A very personal gift denotes a very personal relationship and should be reserved for the intimates on your list.

If your own superior sends you a gift, you are not expected to reciprocate, since a gift to a subordinate, at any level, is a token of appreciation of past performance.

If your firm should send a gift to your home, it is up to your wife – if you have one – to write a note of thanks. She should address the letter to the managing director or whoever was responsible for having the gift sent and, while she alone should sign it, the letter should make some reference to you in the text.

The same rule applies to gifts received from business friends in general. Even if your wife does not know them, it is up to her to write the thank you note. You will then add your thanks verbally when you next meet the donor. If the donor lives in another town and you are not likely to meet him again for several weeks, then you add a paragraph of thanks to your next business letter to him. This, of course, is in addition to your wife's note.

Telephone manners

When you speak on the telephone your voice is your only ally. It alone has the task of conveying to your listener your attitude and your personality – and it does so very accurately. It will therefore pay to cultivate a cheerful and friendly tone of voice, a voice, in fact, with a smile in it, as the G.P.O. so admiringly puts it.

Avoid a dull monotone by modulating your voice. If you have a high-pitched voice, try to pitch it lower, for a voice that rises higher and higher tends to sound hysterical from the other end of a telephone. Purge your voice from all trace of hurry or impatience, for nothing is more nerve-racking than to speak to someone who sounds as if he can't wait to get off the line. Don't be fooled, it *does* get across to your listener.

It is possible to be brief without conveying the feeling of haste, and brevity is, of course, essential in telephone conversations, both for your own sake and that of your listener.

Enunciate clearly, since your listener has only your voice to go

c

by and cannot guess at your meaning by your expression or your gestures, as he would if you were face to face. If your listener cannot understand you, speak more clearly, not more loudly.

Pay close attention to what the other person is saying, since it is very easy though not at all courteous to let your attention wander.

Making a call: It is quicker, cheaper, and more courteous to the person you are calling to dial your own numbers direct. Some companies, however, still have a policy which forces you to get numbers through the switchboard or your secretary. In such a case, ask for your number and get the switchboard or your secretary to give you a ring as soon as the number has been dialled. You can then yourself ask for the person you want. If he is unavailable you will be able to leave a far clearer message than either a switchboard operator or your secretary could.

It is extremely rude to ask your secretary to get a person on the line and then keep him there awaiting your convenience. It is also ill-mannered to expect a person to wait while you rummage through your papers to find something you want to refer to. Avoid this by having such material ready before putting the call through. If you have two or more items to discuss, jot them down beforehand. It is also a good idea to mention how many things you want to discuss, because many people have a way of dashing off the line as soon as one point is settled.

If the subject you want to discuss is a lengthy one, it is courteous to ask the person you are calling whether he has a few moments to discuss it. He may be in the middle of a meeting and grateful of a chance to call you back later.

If you get a wrong number, apologize and hang up. It is quite rude to hang up without a word and irritating if you go into lengthy explanations. If you dial a number and get a crossed wire, hang up at once and dial again. If you are disconnected during a telephone conversation, call the person again at once if you originated the call. If he did, wait for a while and if he does not call back, then do so yourself.

Inter-office calls are also best handled personally, if at all possible. If you have to go through the laborious process of having your secretary dial, then ask her to put you on the line as soon as she has dialled, as this is more courteous to the person you are calling. Even if calling a subordinate you should not keep him waiting unless absolutely unavoidable and it is obviously petty to do so on principle, as it were.

Receiving calls: Answer your telephone promptly. Say who you are or give the name of your department. 'Yes' sounds rather abrupt and 'Hallo' is unbusinesslike. Make sure someone is always available to answer your phone in your absence and make sure they answer it politely. Never fail to call back a person who has left a message in your absence. It is extremely rude not to do so.

Never let an unattended phone go on ringing. Pick up the receiver and say: 'Mr Jones's office' or 'Mr Jones's desk', then offer to take a message.

Always have a pad and pencil near the phone, so that you can jot down messages quickly, without keeping your caller waiting. If it will take you some time to answer your caller's query, offer to ring him back and then do so as expeditiously as possible.

The time-honoured practice of having a secretary ask 'Who's calling?' is really quite rude since it implies that you may be in to some people but not to others. The really courteous executive feels it is a better policy to scrap this practice and risk getting a few unwanted calls. In any event the risk is not very great, since your secretary will soon get to know your regular callers and, with the doubtful ones, she can perhaps say: 'I don't think he's in at the moment, but I'll find out for you. Who shall I say is calling, please?'

If you have any say in the running of the company switchboard, do make sure that calls are answered both courteously and cheerfully. 'Jones and Company, good morning!' in a happy tone of voice is excellent. Also make sure your company telephone-operators do not address callers as 'Dear' – which simply infuriates some people.

The G.P.O. recently put out an excellent little folder called *Making Good Use of the Telephone*. It gives guidance not only on how to handle this increasingly complicated instrument, but also on how to do so courteously.

chapter four

introductions

The in-store Christmas party for the customers' children was drawing to a successful conclusion. It had gone off without a hitch and the delighted, boisterous guests, all 300 of them, were obviously having a good time. Sheila Blake, the department-store public-relations officer who had dreamed up and organized the whole affair, was exhausted yet filled with the satisfaction of a job well done. She had even succeeded in persuading a national television network to attend the party and include it in one of its programmes. They had been interviewing some of the children, photographing them on Father Christmas's lap, fanning the camera over the buffet table and had finally left.

Sheila was just about to go and check once again whether the smaller children were all right when she spotted Keith Manning, the marketing director, coming towards her with a strange man.

'And this,' Manning announced as they reached her, 'is Sheila Blake, our public-relations officer. She tries hard, but achieves nothing.' Having delivered his body blow, Manning went on to introduce the stranger as the new company chairman.

It is quite conceivable that Keith Manning had not the slightest intention of being rude. On another occasion the managing director of a company was introducing one of his executives to the M.D. of a sister company. After mentioning his name, he added: 'He translates all our German correspondence for us, unless it's *too* technical, then we get somebody who *really* knows the language.'

Perhaps this man also had no intention of being rude. Perhaps he was so self-centred that he gave no thought to the feelings of others, which is the essence of good manners.

Yet the rules governing introductions are very simple and every executive can train himself to carry out this simple ceremony expertly and effortlessly every time. The opportunity will present itself almost daily in the businessman's life and it should not be bungled.

The form is that men are introduced to women, juniors to seniors, and both men and women to eminent personages. The two exceptions are that members of your own family are introduced to those outside the family and everyone, whether man or woman, is presented to Royalty.

This means that when introducing two women, you introduce the younger to the elder, or the lower ranking to the higher ranking. It is, of course, often difficult to tell which of any two women is the elder, but rank is usually quite simple. You introduce the new filing clerk *to* her supervisor.

The same applies when introducing two men: the junior ranking is introduced to his senior. Relative rank between people from different companies can, of course, be difficult to judge and, obviously, this rule does not have to be followed to the letter all the way up the hierarchy of a company. You are not expected scrupulously to introduce every salesman to every sales supervisor, every sales supervisor to every sales manager, every sales manager to every marketing manager and so on. In fact, in group introductions the whole thing becomes blurred and you simply introduce the newcomer to everyone else.

The old-fashioned way of effecting introductions was to say: 'May I present Mr So-and-So?' This is no longer done, except in the case of Royalty or in introducing a speaker at a function. Nowadays you simply say: 'John, this is Mr Eldridge. John Brown.' Or: 'Mr Smith, may I introduce Mr Eldridge? Henry Smith.'

It is helpful to add a word of explanation, so that the people being introduced can get their bearings. You might say: 'John, this is Mr Eldridge of White's. John Brown, our sales supervisor.'

There is only one approved reaction to an introduction. Both parties say: 'How d'you do?' and they usually do so together. This is a thoroughly British, nonsensical rule, but it is inviolable and simple. You ask a question that requires no answer and that is that. On no account should you say 'Pleased to meet you' or anything else of this nature.

It is, of course, rather difficult to sound friendly while mumbling a meaningless question, but it helps if you smile and look the other man straight in the eye.

Men always shake hands when introduced and a hearty handshake also helps to take the ice out of the 'How d'you do'? Women are not required to shake hands. They merely smile pleasantly, nod their head and, of course, also say 'How d'you do?' It is considered to be a mark of special friendliness on their part to offer their hand and some of them at least feel compelled to do so to counteract the chill of the meaningless question.

A man rises to acknowledge an introduction. A woman does not. If wearing gloves, a man takes his off before shaking hands. A woman does not.

Remembering names: We all like the sound of our own name, yet we are hopelessly inept at remembering other people's. The Americans, who in many respects have a far greater sense of social obligation than we have, are past-masters at remembering everyone's name and invariably address you by your name immediately upon introduction. If they can do it, so can we. The first and most important step in the right direction is to recognize how important it is to remember and use the name of people we meet.

Once convinced of this fact, it is simply a question of technique. First of all, listen carefully to the name as it is pronounced by the person making the introduction. If you are making the introduction, be sure to pronounce the name distinctly and audibly. When someone has been introduced to you, you can either repeat the name as the Americans do, even though this custom has not yet crossed the Atlantic, or you can comment on it. An American will say: 'Cruikshank? That's an interesting name! How do you spell it?' Or he will say: 'Poldovski? Is that Polish?' If the name is a perfectly simple one, such as Smith or Brown, an American will say: 'How d'you do, Mr Brown?'

This is the secret of how Americans remember names, while we constantly fail to do so, but it is doubtful whether it would be advisable to adopt all of these techniques in Britain, for we are a strange people and would probably take offence at any intelligent attempt to fix our surnames in mind. There remains only the expedient of listening carefully, plus the time-honoured British practice of saying: 'What is your name? I'm afraid I did not catch it.'

As soon after the introduction as possible, jot the name down on a piece of paper and transfer it later to your permanent records. Frequently, you can jot the name down right there and then, when someone is brought into your office, for instance, and then sits down to discuss something with you.

Some people use the association of ideas method to remember names, but it has its pitfalls. It is easy to make the *wrong* association. Writing down the correct name is by far the best method.

If you are the person making the introduction, then remembering the name is not merely useful and friendly, but downright imperative. Yet with the best will in the world, one day you will find yourself about to introduce a person whose name you have completely forgotten. You rack your brain and grow more agitated by the minute, but the more you concentrate the further away in your memory the name seems to recede. People use all sorts of manoeuvres to get themselves out of this situation – for it happens to everyone – but the best thing to do is face up squarely to it and say: 'I'm afraid I've forgotten your name.' No one really takes offence, since this is such a common lapse.

If it is only the man's surname you've forgotten, then you're in a better position. You can just say: 'Silly of me, John, I just can't think of your surname.'

If you sense that someone has forgotten your name while about to introduce you, then bail him out right away to save him the embarrassment of asking. He will be greatly relieved and grateful to you.

Group introductions: This is a situation very frequently encountered in the business world. Simply announce the name of the newcomer and then lead him to each person in the group in turn, saying their names as you go: 'Mr Smith,' 'Mr Brown,' 'Miss Gibbs' and so on.

It frequently happens when introducing one person to a group that everyone knows who the newcomer is, and in such cases it is helpful to add a tag to the name of each person introduced to him. You might say: 'Mr Smith, works manager,' 'Mr Brown, our production manager,' 'Miss Gibbs, my assistant,' and so on down the line.

You are not always so fortunate as to be introducing your own staff, however, and it frequently happens that you are called upon to introduce six or seven people whom you yourself have only just met.

In such a case you can but do your best. Certainly if you know you are going somewhere to meet Messrs A, B, C, D, E, and F, you would do well to write their names down on a small slip of paper, keep it in your jacket pocket and refer to it a couple of times on your way to the rendezvous. You will then find it much easier to connect faces with the names and you should be able to introduce them immediately afterwards to someone else.

It is not necessary in the case of group introductions for everyone to shake hands. 'How d'you do?' with a smile and a bow is sufficient. The handshake, however, is more friendly and there is no reason why it should not be given.

Should you be one of the people in the group and the introducer momentarily forgets your name, simply say 'I'm Joe Doakes. How d'you do?'

Introducing yourself: Quite frequently at a business lunch you may be sitting next to a stranger. Introduce yourself promptly with a: 'I'm Joe Doakes from Flexible Castors.' Your lunch neighbour can then take you up with: 'Oh, yes, I know. You're on the Trading Estate. I'm Henry Smith of the Mutual Trust.' And you're both on your way to a pleasant lunch-time conversation.

You will also want to introduce yourself when others have neglected to do so, for it can be quite embarrassing constantly to come in touch with a person whom someone has failed to introduce. Do the deed yourself and the uncomfortable feeling is dispelled.

Introducing a new employee: The first few days on a job are vital. If a new employee is properly welcomed, introduced to his fellow-workers and his new surroundings and effectively inducted into his new job, the chances of his staying are greatly enhanced. Proper introductions are an extremely important part of this welcoming procedure, yet it is surprising how many companies simply abandon a newcomer to fend for himself on his first day.

A successful applicant for a job should be introduced to his immediate supervisor either at the final interview or immediately upon reporting for work. The supervisor should then introduce the newcomer around. In very small firms, a new employee should meet everyone. In very large firms, he needs to meet only those with whom he will come in daily contact.

It is also very important for employees dealing with people outside the company to get to know them as quickly as possible. This is beneficial not only to the employee, but perhaps even more to the company. A receptionist, for instance, should have someone sitting with her at some time during the first few days to introduce her to the regular callers. In this way important people need never be treated like strangers by an uninitiated employee.

Similarly, a new salesman will have a supervisor with him on his first few days on the road. He can then be introduced to the most important customers and their various idiosyncrasies can be explained to him. This procedure can do a great deal to smooth the way for a new man, while at the same time helping old customers to reconcile themselves to having to deal with a new face.

Introducing a member of your family: The rule about introducing members of your family *to* those outside the family holds good also in business. If you take your wife along to the firm's annual party you will, therefore, introduce her to your colleagues by saying, perhaps, 'Joe, I'd like you to meet my wife. Joan, this is Mr Brown.' If she should go with you to the office, you would introduce her to your secretary right away. You would likewise introduce any member of your family who happened to visit you at the office. If it were your small son, you would simply say: 'Miss Jones, this is Tommy.' If it were your daughter, 'Miss Jones, I'd like you to meet my daughter, Mrs Brown.' However, if your venerable grandmother called in to see you, age would take precedence and you would introduce Miss Jones to her.

Being presented to royalty: Members of the Royal Family frequently visit factories and exhibitions and it is not at all unlikely that one day one of them will visit your stand at an exhibition, or that you will otherwise have occasion to be presented to one or another of them.

People are always presented to royalty. Never the other way around. With royalty, the old-fashioned formula is still used. It goes: 'Your Majesty (or Your Royal Highness) may I present Mr Smith?' Or: 'May I present Mr Smith, Ma'am (or Sir)?' The man then takes the proffered hand and bows his head only – not from the waist. It is customary for women to give a bob-curtsy.

Usually, the person presenting someone to the Queen follows the presentation with some such remark as: 'Mr Smith has been in the steel industry for 25 years.' This gives the Queen an opening to pass some apt remark, but there is absolutely no reason why you should not speak first should the occasion arise.

When asking questions of royalty, it is customary to speak in the third person, e.g. 'Would Your Majesty care to see our new three-phase engines?' Or: 'What did Your Royal Highness think of the exhibition?'

Several members of the Royal Family, especially the Queen and the Queen Mother, have very good memories and it is quite usual for them to remember people who have been presented to them several years earlier.

chapter five

entertaining

Entertaining plays an important role in business and nothing makes a more confident host than a good grounding in the basic facts involved.

Understanding the menu

One of the first stumbling blocks in restaurant entertaining is the menu. In most good restaurants it is written in French and in only a few instances is the English equivalent written underneath. Nothing can therefore be more useful to the non-linguist who aspires to being a good host than a brief study of French culinary terms.

The menu usually gives you the choice of taking the set meal, called *table d'hôte* in Britain, although not in France, or selecting each individual course to your own taste. This latter is called *à la carte*.

Selecting an *à la carte* meal is obviously more difficult for the uninitiated, since it requires a fair understanding of the French terms. It is also almost invariably more expensive than the set meal.

The various dishes are to be found under their corresponding heading as follows:

HORS D'ŒUVRE
variés or *maison*

FIRST COURSE ('STARTER')
both of these mean the usual selection of Russian salad, sardine, egg mayonnaise, anchovy and so on

saumon fumé — smoked salmon

paté de foie gras
paté maison
paté du chef } all of these terms indicate the familiar French delicacy made with goose liver

pamplemousse — grapefruit

melon — melon. Sometimes this is expanded to *melon au jambon de Parme*, meaning melon with thin slices of raw Parma ham

POTAGES
consommé — clear soup

potage
soupe } both of these mean thick soup

soupe à l'oignon — onion soup
potage parmentier — potato soup
potage St Germain — split pea soup
potage paysanne or *à la paysanne* — vegetable soup

crème de .... — this is also thick soup, but always a cream

crème d'asperges — cream of asparagus soup
crème de laitues — cream of lettuce soup
crème portugaise — cream of tomato soup
bisque de homard — lobster soup

POISSONS
merlan — whiting
cabillaud — cod (fresh)
morue — dried, salted cod
bar — bass
blanchailles — whitebait
barbue — brill
colin — hake
merluche — haddock
raie — skate

POISSONS	FISH
turbot	turbot
sole	Dover sole
limande	lemon sole
carrelet or *plie*	plaice
flétan	halibut
hareng	herring
truite	trout
carpe	carp
brochet	pike
anguille	eel

COQUILLAGES	SHELLFISH
huitres	oysters
moules	mussels
coquilles St Jacques	scallops

CRUSTACÉS	also SHELLFISH
homard	lobster
langouste	crayfish
langoustine	Dublin Bay prawns or scampi
crevettes roses	prawns
crevettes grises	shrimps
ecrevisses	freshwater crayfish
crabe	crab

ENTREES

ENTREES
all made-up dishes come under this heading and it is harder to single them out, since veal, for instance, can come either as an entrée or as a roast or grill under the next headings

ROTIS

ROASTS

GRILLADES

GRILLS
the various kinds of meat are as follows and, as indicated, can be found under either of the three preceding headings:

veau	veal
agneau	lamb
bœuf	beef
mouton	mutton
porc	pork

GRILLADES	GRILLS
poulet, volaille	chicken
coq	a cockerel, theoretically at least
poussin	baby chicken
caneton	duckling
canard	duck
oie	goose
dindonneau	young turkey
perdrix	partridge
faisan	pheasant
bécasse	woodcock
caille	quail
pintade	guinea fowl
lièvre	hare

Several words under the same three headings are easily recognizable, i.e. *filet*, fillet, *escalope* and *fricassée*, both adopted into the English language, *braisé*, braised, *bifteck*, meaning beefsteak, and *côtelette*, chop or cutlet. The following are usually found under the heading '*Entrées*':

foie	liver
cervelle	brains
rognon	kidney
ris de veau	veal sweetbread
tête de veau	calf's head

In this main part of the menu there are usually also one or more *plâts du jour*, meaning the special dish of the day. In the more expensive restaurants, vegetables are charged for separately. In the less expensive restaurants they are included in the price of the main dish and in this case the menu reads, for instance: *Escalope de veau garnie*, escalope of veal with vegetables. This expression, however, is used more in France than in English restaurants. Vegetables are listed as follows:

LEGUMES	VEGETABLES
pommes de terre (often abbreviated to *pommes*)	potatoes
chouxfleur	cauliflower
haricots verts	French beans

LEGUMES	VEGETABLES
petits pois	peas
épinards	spinach
choux de Bruxelles	Brussels sprouts
choux	cabbage
carottes	carrots
céléri	celery
artichaut	globe artichoke
tobinambour	Jerusalem artichoke
tomate	tomato
aubergine	egg plant

Fromages is the heading for cheeses and puddings come under *Desserts* or *Entremets*, as follows:

pommes	apples
poires	pears
pêches	peaches
abricots	apricots
cerises	cherries
raisins	grapes
fraises	strawberries
groseilles à grappes	red or white currants
groseilles vertes	gooseberries
framboises	raspberries
prunes	plums
pruneaux	prunes
glace	ice cream

Under this heading also there are a number of familiar terms, such as *tarte, soufflé, gâteau,* and *pâtisserie* which means pastry in general.

For some reason, restaurants which think of themselves as being the absolute best prefix every item on the menu with the corresponding article, so that the headings would read: *Les Hors d'Oeuvre, Les Potages, Les Poissons,* and so on. Each individual dish would also have its appropriate handle, such as, *Le Rôti de Boeuf au Jus,* which is none other than The Roast Beef of Old England.

Very little study is required to master at least the rudiments of culinary French and the rest can be learnt by constant observation. The only serious drawback to the observation technique is that very few restaurants actually prepare a dish as it should be prepared.

When in doubt, no stigma attaches to asking the waiter what this or that dish is. Obviously, however, your guests would put you down as not being much of a man of the world if you were caught asking what the *Rôti de Bœuf* was. Ultimately, there is no cure for ignorance but education and the pig's ear attempting to pass himself off as a silk purse is deceiving no one but himself.

Selecting the wines

The second pitfall lying in wait for the unwary host is the selection of wines to accompany the food. It is the host's prerogative to choose the wine, even though sometimes out of courtesy he will ask his guests what kind of wine they like.

It takes almost a lifetime to become a connoisseur of good wine and there is no short cut to acquiring this most civilized and satisfying accomplishment. The basic rudiments, however, are not hard to grasp.

Sherry: This is perhaps the most familiar wine drunk in Britain. It is a blended wine made from grapes grown in the Jerez district of Spain. Sherry ranges all the way from very dry to very sweet and full-bodied, the difference being achieved through the use of different types of grapes in different blends. Manzanilla is the driest of dry sherry. Amontillado and Fino are medium-dry and a light amber in colour. Oloroso and Amoroso are sweet, rich, and darker in colour.

Port: This is also a blended wine, made from grapes grown in the Douro River valley in northern Portugal. There are ports of every shade of colour and every degree from dry to sweet. When a port is young it is a deep purple colour and is known as 'Full'. It grows gradually paler as it ages, becoming first 'Ruby' and then 'Tawny'. Ruby port is a robust wine, rich and satisfying. Tawny port is lighter and mellower. White port is made from white grapes.

Madeira: Madeira is a fortified wine, but unlike sherry and port, it is not blended. Each type of grape produces its corresponding wine, much as usually happens with table wines. Sercial is a dry Madeira, quite different in taste from sherry. Verdelho is a soft wine, slightly green in colour and less dry than Sercial. Bual and Malmsey are full-bodied, sweet after-dinner wines.

Claret: Claret, or Bordeaux, is a table wine made from grapes grown in the Gironde Département of South-west France. There are both red and white Bordeaux, from dry to sweet. The red Bordeaux are: Médoc, Haut-Médoc, Margaux, Moulis, Listrac, Saint-Julien, Pauillac, Saint Esthèphe, and Graves, which are grown on the right bank of the river Dordogne, and Saint-Emilion, Pomerol, Fronsac, Blayais, Bourgeais, Premières Côtes de Bordeaux, and Côtes de Castillon, which are grown on the left bank.

The dry white clarets are Graves and Entre-Deux-Mers. The sweet are: Sauternes, Barsac, Cérons, Loupiac, and Ste-Croix-du-Mont. The following are mellow, that is, a little less dry than dry: Premières Côtes de Bordeaux, Saint-Macaire, Graves de Vayre, Haut-Benauge, Sainte-Foy, and Blaye et Bourg.

Burgundy: The only true burgundies are those produced in the Burgundian vineyards of France. Some of the outstanding ones are: Chablis, a very dry white wine, produced in the North of Burgundy; Chambertin, Nuits Saint-Georges, and Clos de Vougeot, all from the Côte de Nuits in the North; Corton and Pommard, two smooth, velvety wines from the Côte de Beaune; Meursault and the various Montrachet wines, made from white Chardonnay grapes; Pouilly-Fuissé from the Macon region and the light and lively wines of Beaujolais.

Unfortunately both the generic term 'Burgundy' and several of the names of individual wines such as Chablis have been 'borrowed' by other countries and attached to their own wines, so that we now hear about Spanish Burgundies and Chilean Chablis. In point of fact, even if a vine is taken from France and transplanted elsewhere, the resulting wine will be different, since the quality and character of a wine depend not only on the vine which has produced it, but also on the soil it has grown in, its cultivation, the climate, and the way it has been made.

D

It would, therefore, have been far better for each country to introduce its own wine under its own name and allow it to make its own reputation, for good or for bad. As it is, the so-called burgundies produced by other countries are darker and heavier than the real thing, while Chilean wines, though excellent, are far lighter than the German wines whose names they appropriate. As for the many 'port-type' wines produced, the least said the better.

Fortunately, it is perfectly simple to recognize a bottle of genuine fine French wine by its label, since each is given the name of its place of origin. This *appellation d'origine*, as it is called in French, is very strictly controlled and every label is clearly marked '*Appellation Controlée*'. Since the *appellation d'origine* may only be used for wines made according to local practice in the place named on the label, it gives you a double guarantee: of origin and quality.

This very elementary division between a genuine fine French wine bottled in France and the rest is quite simple and accessible even to the merest beginner, but to go beyond this requires application over a long period of time, since each of the various vineyards within a given region produces different wines of varying degrees of excellence and each, of course, is sold under its own particular name. The finest go by the name of their own estate, variously called Château, Clos, Domaine, or Crus. Chambertin Clos de Bèze, for instance, is the famous wine of Napoleon, and is produced in a vineyard of no more than 50 acres.

Hock and Moselle: These are the white wines of the Rhineland. The finest hocks are frequently qualified as *Spaetlese* (late-gathered), *Auslese* (selected), or *Beerenauslese* (over-ripe selected), all three types being on the sweet side. Hocks improve with age, are more alcoholic and have more body than Moselles, which are best drunk when young.

These two wines are easily distinguished by the colour of their bottles: brownish for Moselles and dark-green for Hocks.

Champagne: The only true champagne is that which hails from the Champagne district, East of Paris. It is a blended, sparkling wine, made according to a special process called the *méthode champenoise*. The leading brands are Veuve Cliquot, Bollinger,

Pommery et Gréno, Perrier-Jouet, Mumm, Moët et Chandon, and Heidsieck.

There are many other excellent sparkling wines, such as Asti Spumante, made from Moscato grapes in the true *champenoise* fashion. This wine comes from the vineyards of Piedmont, in Northern Italy, which yield so many other excellent wines.

Brandy: Brandy is a spirit distilled from wine. The finest and most famous of them all is Cognac, made from Charente wine in the Cognac district of France. No other brandy has a right to be called Cognac. All brandies which come under the official designation of Cognac are registered by the *Bureau National Interprofessionnel du Cognac.* New brandy is entered in the 'O' register and moves up to the next register each year for the first five years of its life and remains in the '5' register until marketed.

One-star brandy is not less than three years old; two-star four years old; three-star five years old. v.s.o.p., Very Special Old Pale, indicates a brandy between eighteen and twenty-four years old.

Armagnac is the oldest of the French brandies, although it is less well-known abroad than Cognac. Other countries, notably Spain, also make excellent brandies.

France produces many other wines apart from the world-famous Burgundies, Bordeaux, and Champagne. Each part of France, in fact, has its own special wine and, at least when travelling, the best thing to do is to drink the local wine.

As already mentioned, Italy, too, produces many excellent wines, some of them world-renowned. The most famous outside Italy is undoubtedly Chianti, in the familiar straw-covered flask. The name '*Chianti*' is not legally protected, such as, for instance, the word '*Cognac*', and many wine merchants have taken advantage of this fact to call their dubious wines *Chianti*, thereby cashing in on the popularity of the true *Chianti* at the expense of the uninformed public. If you should want to order a bottle of *Chianti*, therefore, make sure it carries one of two seals: either a black cockerel on a golden background, which means that the wine is produced in a carefully-defined region extending over 150,000 acres between Florence and Siena; or a white *putto* (cherub), which means that the wine, while not the real 'classical' *Chianti*, is very little different from it and was produced in a district surrounding that which produces the *Chianti classico*.

Many other countries produce their own wines, some of which are imported into this country. Even the Americas produce their own wines but, apart from Chilean wines and a few Californian ones, the wines from the New World do not begin to compare with European ones.

How and when to serve wines

Wine is a living thing and requires careful handling. Dry white and rosé wines should be served cool, but not iced. Sweet wines should be a little cooler. Red wines should be served at room temperature. They should be brought to this temperature naturally, by allowing them to stand in the room for at least twenty-four hours. On no account should they be forcibly heated by standing them in front of the fire or in warm water, although, lamentably, many restaurants actually do this. Allow the wine to breathe and develop in the air by uncorking it an hour or two before serving.

Some red wines require decanting because of the sediment lying at the bottom of the bottle.

Champagne and other sparkling wines should be served chilled. The bottle should be placed in the refrigerator or in a bucket of water and ice an hour before serving. A wine should never be served too cold, as this destroys its delicate flavour. Never put ice in wine.

The marriage of food and wine

The art of marrying food with the most suitable wine is one of the most civilized and exquisite pleasures. The wine should complement and enhance the flavour of the food it accompanies. It should be a foil to the food, matching it in delicacy or robustness of flavour. There are no hard and fast rules for selecting the right wines. Your criterion should be your own taste.

Do not deaden your taste buds by drinking hard liquor before

a meal. A glass of sherry or Madeira will do far more to prepare
your palate for the pleasures of the table. Afterwards serve your
wines in this order: the poor before the great, the light before
the heavy, the dry before the sweet and the young before the
old.

As for individual choice for the various courses, you might like
to try some of the following:

With hors d'œuvre	Dry sherry or white Bordeaux
With oysters, lobster and other shellfish	Chablis, Pouilly, Dry Graves, Alsatian wine, or dry Champagne
With fried or grilled fish	Moselle or dry white Bordeaux or Burgundy
With salmon, turbot or sole served with a sauce	Have the conventional dry white wine or try one of the great rich Sauternes, such as Château Yquem
With light entrées, such as blanquettes, fricassées or gammon	Try a delicate, light wine such as Beaujolais or a white Bordeaux
With roast or grilled meat:	
Veal, Lamb or Pork	A light Bordeaux, such as St Julien, Margaux, or St-Estèphe
Beef or Mutton	These deserve the best vintage red wines, such as Côtes de Nuits, Côte de Beaune, or Côte du Rhône
Poultry	A light red Bordeaux or a dry white burgundy
Dessert	Sauterne, Hock, a rich Champagne or sparkling Moselle
Fruit and Nuts	A great Sauterne, Madeira or a brown sherry
Cheese and wine seem to be made for each other. Many delightful combinations can be made. In general, follow the rule: mild cheese with light wine, strong cheese with robust wine. For instance:	
Soft cream cheeses	Dry white, dry Madeira or light rosé wine

Hard, firm cream cheese	Dry white, rosé, or light red wine
Blue-veined cheeses	Port or full-bodied red wine
With coffee	Serve brandy or liqueurs

Champagne and Hock can accompany any course.

Table manners

Table manners are mostly conventions arrived at for no particular reason and which benefit no one, but with a smattering of good habits which take into account the feelings and comfort of your fellow diners. The latter are very important indeed and, like all matters pertaining to good manners, are applicable throughout the civilized world. These good habits include eating with your mouth closed where at all possible, eating silently, keeping your elbows close to your sides so as not to poke at your neighbour, refraining from smoking until the meal is finished and not speaking of subjects unsuited to meal times, such as operations and so on.

The plethora of other 'do's' and 'don'ts' vary from country to country. The young executive with his eye to the top of the managerial ladder would do well to follow them, but it would be quite unwise and, indeed, foolish, to take them too seriously like the man in Thackeray's *Book of Snobs* who cut a man dead for eating peas with a knife, only to discover later that he had spent fifteen years as a political prisoner and had been given only a two-pronged fork to eat with.

The approved British eating drill is as follows: begin the meal by shaking out your table napkin and placing it across your lap – unless the waiter has already done it for you. You will find the cutlery placed in the order in which you will need to use it, so that assuming a meal of soup, fish, meat, and dessert you will find on your right, moving from the outside in: soup spoon, fish knife, meat knife. On your left: fish fork, meat fork. In most restaurants, dessert spoon and fork and bread knife are placed one below the other at the top of the cover.

In a restaurant, if you have not ordered the fish, for instance, the waiter will remove the fish knife and fork, thus clearing up the confusion a little. If you have none the less used the wrong implement and find yourself with nothing but a butter knife with which to tackle your steak, simply motion the waiter over and ask for a steak knife.

Salt and mustard should be placed on the side of the plate, never sprinkled directly on to the food. This enjoinder must obviously be disregarded, however, in the case of the salt mills which have recently appeared on the British table.

Butter and jam must likewise be placed on the side of the plate, never directly on to the bread. Salads go on the special salad plate, if provided, otherwise on to the meat plate. You are actually free to put sauces and gravy either on the food or on the side, but mashing your food in it is taboo.

Between mouthfuls, rest knife and fork across your plate, roughly at right-angles to each other. On no account should you rest them on the table cloth. When you have finished a course, place knife and fork neatly together on your plate. This indicates to the waiter that you have finished. There are supposed to be two schools of thought on whether the tines of the fork and the bowl of the spoon should be turned upwards or downwards, but this momentous question surely does not merit undue attention.

The various edibles should be tackled as follows:

Apples and pears   On formal occasions, these should be speared with the fork, cut into quarters, cored and peeled, then cut into smaller pieces and eaten with fruit knife and fork. At more down-to-earth occasions, this fruit is usually eaten with the fingers after cutting and coring.

Artichokes   They are served either hot with an individual dish of melted butter, or cold with a dish of vinaigrette. Lift off each leaf, dip the edible tip in the sauce provided and bite it off. Lift the small white leaves left in the centre and scrape away the choke below them. Eat the heart with a knife and fork.

Asparagus   The eating of asparagus has inspired no end of amusing stories and anecdotes. One of them suggests that King Edward VII was in complete agreement with the statement that consideration for the feelings of others is far more important than mere etiquette. The King was entertaining a distinguished guest from India at dinner. Asparagus had been served and the King noticed his Indian guest eating the asparagus tip, then tossing the inedible part over his shoulder. Promptly the King proceeded to do likewise and the other diners followed suit, thereby saving the stranger from possible embarrassment.

Asparagus is actually the simplest thing to eat, inasmuch as it is eaten with the fingers. It is usually served with melted butter or a sauce. Simply pick up the asparagus with your fingers, dip the green tip into the butter or other sauce provided, bite off the tip, then place the hard inedible part on the side of your plate. If the asparagus is very thin and over-cooked, there is nothing to stop you from using a fork, and this, in fact, is the more modern practice. Many American restaurants supply tongs with which to pick up asparagus.

Avocado pear It is served halved, with the stone removed and the hollow filled with a sauce, vinaigrette, prawns, crab, or with lemon which you squeeze into the pear. Eat it with a spoon.

Caviare It is served with toast, butter, and lemon. Butter the toast, squeeze lemon on the caviare, and pile a mouthful at a time on to the toast, which you then eat with your fingers.

Cheese Soft cheese is spread on to biscuit or bread, hard cheese is balanced, a mouthful at a time, on to biscuit or bread. The Continental practice of eating cheese with a knife and fork is gaining popularity.

Corn on the cob There is no elegant way of eating this vegetable. It is sometimes served with a skewer stuck into each end. In such cases, pick it up by the skewers with both hands and bite off the corn from end to end. You will have previously spread the corn with butter and added salt and pepper to taste. If no skewers are provided, just pick up the cob with your fingers and go to town.

Curry Curry is served with a spoon and fork. Eat it as you would a pudding.

Grapes and cherries Deposit the pips and cherry stones into your closed fist and funnel them on to your plate. If the cherries are cooked, you can sometimes separate the stones while on the plate. Otherwise, remove them from your mouth on to your spoon.

Gulls' eggs   They are served hard-boiled in their shells, four or five to a dish or basket. Pick one up, crack it on the side of your plate, shell it, dip it into salt and eat it with your fingers.

Jelly   Eat it with spoon and fork or spoon alone. Never with fork alone.

Lobster   It is usually served in the half-shell, with claws and mayonnaise nearby. Eat the lobster with your fish knife and fork, or fork only, dipping each piece into the sauce. Hold claw in your left hand and dig flesh out with the special lobster pick provided, or with your fish fork.

Melon   Whether a half melon or a slice it is served with sugar, ground ginger, cinnamon, lemon, or draped with thinly-sliced Parma ham. Sprinkle the melon with the condiments provided and eat it with a spoon if a half or with spoon and fork or knife and fork if a slice.

Mussels   They are served in a dish in their own broth. The most formal way of eating them is to use fork and spoon, forking the fish on to the spoon and eating it together with a little of the broth. The slightly less formal way is to pick up the shells with your fingers and take out the mussel with your fork, finally drinking the broth with a spoon. The French way of dealing with the situation is to use one half-shell as a spoon, scoop out each mussel with it, and eat it with a little of the broth. The remaining broth is mopped up with bread. It is difficult to imagine an Englishman indulging in such an eminently sensible and enjoyable procedure.

Olives   Use fingers if no *hors d'œuvre* picks are provided. If there is a stone in it, transfer it into your closed fist and from there on to your plate or the nearest suitable receptacle.

Orange   Spear it with a fork held in the left hand,

quarter it and peel it with your knife, separate the segments, remove the pips and eat the segments one at a time. On less grand occasions it is more usual to use fingers and knife for this tricky operation.

Oysters

They are served by the dozen or half-dozen, on the half-shell around a plate, sometimes on ice. They are accompanied by brown bread and butter, lemon and red pepper. Squeeze the lemon on the oysters, sprinkle on some red pepper and eat them with the special fork provided. On less grand occasions, it is perfectly in order to drink the juice from the shell, if you like it.

Pâté de foie gras

It is served with toast. Spread the pâté on the toast, a mouthful at a time.

Prawns

If served in their shells, shell them with your fingers and dip them in the accompanying sauce. If they are served already shelled, eat them with a fork.

Peaches

Spear with a fork held in left hand and peel with a fruit knife. Cut small pieces from around the stone and eat them with the fork.

Peas

Hold the fork in your left hand with the tines pointing downwards, then press the peas against the back of the fork with your knife. You will unhappily find that some peas are too hard for this treatment.

Scallops

They are served in their own shell. Eat them with a fork.

Snails

This French delicacy can be a dangerous trap for the unwary. A delicious story has been making the rounds in Soho. It concerns a couple busily eating their snails at one of London's top restaurants. Suddenly the lady missed her grip and the red-hot snail jumped up in the air and landed down her decolleté. She screamed hysterically, too distraught to take action. Her escort, no more than a distant friend, was paralysed with embarrassment. Suddenly he seized a passing waiter by the arm and implored: 'For God's sake do something, waiter.' Without a word, the waiter inserted finger and thumb between the lady's cleavage and extracted the errant snail. He then discreetly disappeared, never to be seen again.

But to get back to our snails: they are served six or a dozen to a special round dish and a pair of tongs and two-pronged fork are provided. Seize each shell with the tongs in the left hand and extract the snail with the special fork. It is perfectly in order to turn the shell upside down to let out all the garlic butter, which is then mopped up with bread.

Spaghetti

The only correct way to eat spaghetti is with a fork only, held in the right hand. Stick the fork sideways into the spaghetti, twirl a reasonable amount around the fork and eat them. Don't panic if some of the spaghetti refuse to be docile. It happens all the time in Italy. You simply coax them with the greatest nonchalance into your mouth. In spite of the number of people who do it, it is not correct to twirl your spaghetti around a spoon held in the left hand. This is classified as a *petit bourgeois* habit in Italy and if you do not wish to be branded as such, don't do it! It makes it no easier, anyhow. And, of course, spaghetti are plural.

Soup

Soup served in a plate should be taken from the side of the spoon. Tilt the plate away from you to take the last drops. Clear soup served in a cup may be drunk out of the cup or with a spoon. Usually, one takes a few spoonfuls and then, when it is cool enough, the rest of the consommé is drunk from the cup.

Rolls

Rolls should be broken and buttered piece by piece.

Whitebait

Squeeze lemon on the tiny fish and eat them whole, head and all. Accompany with bread and butter.

Business luncheons large and small

If you are simply taking one or two clients or prospective clients to lunch, there is hardly any problem at all. You will want to take the precaution of booking a table in advance, to make sure your guests are not inconvenienced, and if you are meeting them there, you will naturally want to arrive ahead of time to welcome them.

It is thoughtful to give guests some slight guidance in making their selection from the menu, as they may not be sure whether to settle for the less expensive set meal or whether they can feel free to lash out with the lobster thermidor. A good way of doing this is to say, for instance: 'I *can* recommend their steaks, if you feel like that sort of thing.' Or: 'Do you fancy some duck, or are you more of a roast-beef man?' If you are in the unfortunate position of being under doctor's orders to eat lightly, it would be thoughtful to say something like: 'I'm afraid I shall have to stick to an omelette by doctor's orders, but why don't you try a steak, or perhaps the lobster?' Such thoughtfulness puts guests at ease and encourages them to order what they really like.

When it comes to ordering the wine, you can ask your guests if they have any preferences and then do your best from the wine list, discreetly enlisting the wine-waiter's help if you need it. No real connoisseur would ever hesitate to enlist the help of one more knowledgeable than he, so why should you? If, on the other hand, one of your guests is known to you as a connoisseur of wine, then by all means ask him if he would care to select the wine. He will be flattered and glad to perform this pleasurable service.

When the time comes to pay the bill, you will check it over quickly, but you won't quibble over every item, for nothing is more embarrassing to a guest than to have his host haggle over the bill. Tip the waiter between 10 and 15 per cent of the bill, according to the grade of restaurant. Some of the first-class London restaurants have recently started adding a 12½ per cent service charge to the bill, thereby simplifying the tipping problem for their customers. In restaurants where the joints are wheeled around on a trolley and carved in front of the diners, the carver usually expects a tip of about a shilling.

If you do a great deal of business entertaining, you will find it more convenient to have a standing account with one or two favourite restaurants. This will facilitate the bill-paying process and spare your guests even the slightest embarrassment. Credit

'. . . a tendency to drag. . . .'

cards are another very convenient way of taking care of business entertaining.

Sometimes the business lunch or dinner will be different in some way. You may, for instance, have two or three guests from abroad and in this case you will want to give special attention to their comfort. If you do not speak their language well, it would be thoughtful to invite a member of your staff who does to accompany you or, if mutual understanding threatens to be nil, you will invite along the interpreter you have hired for the business talks.

There is often a tendency to drag visitors from abroad around to suit one's self and since they cannot protest, they often find themselves doing things they don't want to do and going to places in which they have no interest. So make a special effort to find out what they *really* want to do, rather than imposing your wishes on them.

Not infrequently, they have special preferences in food and drink and you should do everything you can to please them in this respect. People from some countries are not accustomed to rushing over a meal as we sometimes do and it is thoughtful to remember this when entertaining friends from abroad.

In the case of a larger party with two or three visitors from abroad, you will obviously try to seat each of them next to someone who speaks their language. Also bear in mind that a smile and a warm manner alone go a long way to conveying your pleasure at being with them.

Another slightly different situation occurs when women are present at a business lunch or dinner. If the women are simply executives from your own company, you proceed as you normally would with men and women guests, but sometimes you may be entertaining a woman guest of honour, perhaps a customer, or you may have one or two women executive guests. In this event it is essential that you take care of your guest of honour and the other women properly, for while women executives are well accustomed to being in a minority among men, they do greatly appreciate a little thoughtfulness when they are being entertained. And if the guest of honour is, perhaps, a housewife being fêted for some reason or other, the whole performance will probably be bewildering to her and you may well defeat the object of the exercise if you do not do everything in your power to put her at her ease.

If, for instance, you are all gathered in the bar having a drink and the head-waiter comes in to tell you your table is ready, it would be thoughtful of you to turn to your guest of honour and say: 'Shall we go in to lunch, Mrs Jones?' If there are one or two other women in the party, it would also be courteous to have instructed two other male members of the party to take in the other women.

This procedure is unquestionably the most thoughtful way to handle a situation of this sort, even though it is more formal than is currently the mode, because it will both put your perhaps shy guest of honour at her ease and please the other women.

You will then seat your guest of honour on your right and indicate where your other guests should sit. If you have little confidence in your memory or presence of mind, you can always use place cards. You will of course make sure that the other women are seated at suitable intervals around the table.

If your guest of honour is very shy and unknowledgeable, you can do a lot to help her along and decide what she should do and she will be most grateful to you.

If there are women in the party, whether members of your own firm or outside guests, it thoughtful to draw them into the party, as it were, making sure they have a drink and keeping them in the conversation. It is surprising how frequently men abandon women guests in a corner with a drink, while they huddle together over the bar or elsewhere. This is extremely thoughtless and embarrassing to a woman. It is always up to the majority to give thought to those in a minority and this applies not only to women, but also to other minorities, whoever they may be.

If your guest of honour is a man, then you also give him your special attention and seat him to your right at the table, assuming that there is no hostess.

Banquets and large parties

The company chairman slipped into the dining-room to make sure all was in order for the banquet. The waiters were just putting out the oysters. 'What, only half a dozen each?' he asked.

'That's right, sir,' the head-waiter replied.

'Oh, well, serve me a dozen,' the chairman instructed. '*I'm* the chairman.'

Perhaps this company chairman was a splendid organizer, but

his manners were certainly deplorable. Serving the host a dozen oysters and his guests only half was too much even for the head-waiter and he instructed the waiters to offer an additional half-dozen also to the guests.

But there is a lot of work involved in organizing a banquet before reaching the oyster stage. It is as well to see what happens at a purely social dinner, since there are obviously points of similarity between a social function and a business one.

At very formal social dinners, as at Buckingham Palace or at embassy dinners, each gentleman is informed upon arrival which lady he will take in to dinner. This is often done by presenting the gentleman with a small envelope with his name on it, containing a card with a lady's name on it. After greeting his host and hostess, it is the gentleman's duty to seek out the lady he is to take in.

When dinner is announced, the host leads the way into the dining-room, escorting the most important woman guest; the hostess follows with the most important male guest, or lets the other couples go in and brings up the rear with her escort. Place-cards indicate where everyone is to sit. The most important woman guest is seated to the host's right, the second most important woman guest on his left. The most important male guest sits to the hostess's right and the second most important man to her left.

The gentlemen pull out the chairs for their ladies and make sure they are comfortably seated before taking their own places. The hostess is seated last of all, but gives the signal for beginning to eat, usually by starting herself.

When the meal is over, the hostess catches the eye of the principal woman guest and rises. All the other women follow suit and retire to the drawing-room. The gentlemen rise, one of them opening the door for the ladies and then sit more closely together, the host usually taking over the seat vacated by the hostess to talk to the principal male guest. The port is passed around clockwise and after twenty minutes or so the host suggests joining the ladies in the drawing-room.

Normally, however, even at Buckingham Palace, the ladies lead the way in to dinner, followed by the men. The custom of the women leaving at the end of a meal, while still practised in a number of households, is also dying out. The host normally simply tells his guests where they are to sit from his place at the head of the table.

The differences between a purely social formal dinner as described and a large business dinner or banquet, are three:

1 First of all there are very seldom as many women as men at business dinners.

2 There is usually no hostess at a business function, which completely alters the seating procedure.

3 Business dinners are rarely, if ever, purely social occasions and seating arrangements have to be modified accordingly.

At a large business dinner, then, if one table suffices for everyone, the chief executive will take the head of the table, the principal guest will sit on his right, the next most important guest on his left and the remaining guests will alternate with other company executives. If there are ladies present they, of course, will alternate as far as possible with the men.

For larger parties, numbering up to one hundred, the table arrangement shown in Fig. 1 is very sociable and practical. Still

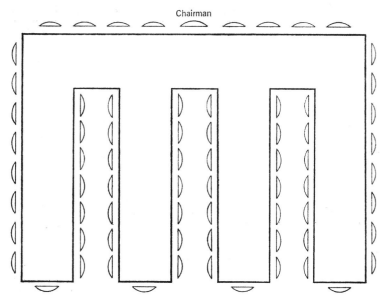

Fig. 1 Seating Arrangements

E

larger functions call for a head table and several general tables, either round or long, as shown in Fig. 2. Functions of this size usually have one or more speakers on the programme, someone has to preside, and if there are important guests, seating arrange-

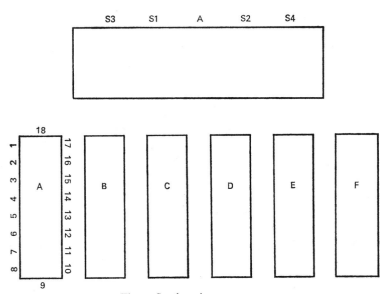

Fig. 2 Seating Arrangements

KEY

Head Table

A Chairman, toast master or M.C.
S1 Principal speaker
S2 Second speaker
S3 Third speaker
S4 Fourth speaker

Table A

1 Mr George White
2 Miss Merrill Smith
3 Mr Felix Wallace (*et seq.*)

Table B

1 Mr Robert Green
2 Miss Jane Blackwell (*et seq.*)

ments have to be carefully made according to the right order of precedence. Careful planning is also needed to enable everyone to find his allotted seat easily.

At city or borough functions, the Lord Mayor or Mayor will preside. At company functions, it will usually be the managing director who, as chairman, will occupy the centre seat at the head table (Figs. 1 and 2). If there is only one speaker, he will sit on the chairman's right. If there are two, the principal speaker will sit on the chairman's right and the second speaker on his left. A third speaker would sit next to the first speaker and a fourth next to the second speaker (Fig. 2). If the principal speaker's wife is present, she might be placed on the chairman's right, with the speaker on his left. In fact, unless Royalty is present, the principal speaker's place is invariably next to the chairman. However, if distinguished guests are invited and one of them is better known than the second speaker, the guest will sit on the chairman's left and the second speaker next to him.

At many company-sponsored dinners there is, of course, usually only one speaker and no invited guests, in which case, obviously, other company executives and senior employees are invited to sit at the head table.

When distinguished guests are invited, attention must be given to precedence, bearing in mind that their relative importance is, to some extent, judged by their distance from the head table. The correct order of precedence is given in Chapter 8. Otherwise, consult *Whitaker's Almanack*. The Lord Lieutenant of the County deals with inquiries regarding county dignitaries and his secretary is usually a mine of information. The Marshal of the Diplomatic Corps at the Foreign Office, Downing Street, London, S.W.1, deals with inquiries regarding foreign diplomats and individual embassies will also help. If the function concerns personnel of local authorities, the Town Clerk, Lord Mayor or Mayor's office, local squire, vicar or editor of the local newspaper are useful sources of information.

At purely business functions, it is advisable not to be overawed by titles of nobility. At such a function, Lord Such would be invited in his capacity of chairman of the Nuts and Bolts Company and should be seated accordingly. Similarly, it would be foolish to invite Lord Such-and-Such to the head table just because of his title, when his position in the company is that of management trainee. For just as there are no men and women in business, so there are no commoners and nobility.

At a Company or Society dinner, care should be taken to seat one prominent guest next to each top executive or leading member of the Society. Wives and husbands should be separated and if there are very few women, they should be rationed out, one or two to a table.

When the seating plan is complete, have place-cards made out in duplicate for everyone sitting at the head table. Each card will be numbered starting from the left, facing the general tables. The appropriate card will then be handed to each invited guest as he arrives.

As for the general tables, each one will be given a letter of the alphabet and numbered place-cards will be used. A large copy of the seating plan will then be displayed in one or more prominent positions – perhaps one in the room where cocktails are served before the meal and another one just outside the dining-room. The diners' names will be listed on the seating plan under the appropriate table, as follows:

Table A
1 Mr George White
2 Miss Merrill Smith
3 Mr Felix Wallace

and so on, as indicated in Fig. 2.

Of course, at many large functions, guests sit where they like and this obviates the need for a table plan. In other instances, such as at a sales conference lunch or dinner, a company executive is placed at the head and foot of each table and the 'foot-soldiers' sit where they like.

If you are presiding at a dinner and there are several unfamiliar faces at the head table, it will pay you to have a small table plan by you with the names written in. This will enable you to identify everyone instantly as he speaks and to call him by name without the slightest difficulty.

Dances

'What dance is this?' the young man asked, after he had led his partner half way across the floor.

'A fox-trot,' she replied, not a little displeased with him.

'Then we shall trot like foxes,' the young man replied, feeling terribly clever. It would probably have surprised him to learn that, far from being clever, he was being quite rude. It is, in fact, an impertinence to ask a lady to dance without knowing even what the dance is, let alone how to dance it. Thus a knowledge of the rudiments of social dancing is an accomplishment which no rising executive can afford to be without.

Imagine, for instance, a young executive asking the chairman's wife for a dance at the annual company party. If he stumps around the floor like a bear, treads on her toes and pumps her arm up and down like a yokel at the village hop, he will obviously give a bad impression. When his name crops up in private conversation with her husband, the chairman's wife is quite apt to say: 'Oh, young Jones? I didn't really think very much of *him*.'

Imagine further the sales manager of a large manufacturing concern who has been trying for the past three months to land a very important contract. Negotiations have reached the final stages and two of the top executives of the prospective client company have come to London to visit the factory. They have been very much impressed with what they have seen and are now being entertained at one of the most exclusive night clubs. One of the men has brought his wife, who wanted an excuse to do some shopping in London.

Our sales manager had never been interested in anything so frivolous as dancing and certainly could not tell the difference between a waltz and a fox-trot. But obviously he had to ask the lady to dance and ask her he did. The other two men, with very little interest in dancing, looked on and before their eyes they saw the suave, silver-tongued, confident man they had known turned into a clumsy, ill-at-ease yokel. His image of self-assured efficiency had fallen from him and he stood revealed in all his awkward social inadequacy. Perhaps he won the contract just the same, but as a man of the world he stood diminished.

The moral is, of course, learn to dance. It is not necessary for a businessman to glide across a dance floor like a gold medallist and all he needs to do is master what dancing schools call 'social rhythm'. Quick and slow 'rhythm', plus the waltz, will permit the businessman to acquit himself with honour in any situation.

There are very few points of etiquette left in connection with dancing. Ladies no longer have 'cards' which need filling up, except, apparently, in Scotland. Gentlemen no longer wear gloves at dances, except for old-time dancing.

The points to bear in mind boil down to three:

1 When at a dance – dance. Nothing is more exasperating for a woman to want to dance and to be obliged instead to sit down while the men hang around the bar discussing the 2.30 race. At a staff dance, the company brass should dance with as many of the girls as they can, not sit together and spend the evening dancing with one another's wives. At dances in general, the first and last dance is owed to the lady you take along. At dances where royalty is present, you may not dance with the royal ladies unless presented to them. If this happens, then you *must* do so, for this is generally the very reason for the introduction.

2 You ask for a dance in one of many ways, from the formal: 'May I have the pleasure of this dance?' to simply: 'Shall we dance?' according to the degree of acquaintance with the lady in question. In asking royalty, you would say 'May I have the honour of this dance, Ma'am?'

3 When the dance is over you say 'Thank you' and escort your partner back to her seat. The really gallant men even manage a little bow at this stage, but they are in the minority. In fact, far too many men these days turn their heels and abandon their partner in the middle of the dance floor. A most deplorable habit.

chapter six

being a desirable guest

As a businessman, you probably do a fair amount of entertaining, but you will also not infrequently be on the receiving end of the entertainment and you will be just as anxious to play your part equally well as a guest.

In the case of a formal invitation, the first thing you will want to do is answer it correctly and this subject is dealt with at length in Chapter 9.

Correct attire and decorations

Some years ago, when Joseph Kennedy was appointed Ambassador to the Court of St James, he appeared at Buckingham Palace to present his credentials attired in a tweed suit. No doubt he thought that he was expressing his contempt for convention and displaying a fearless, freedom-loving mind. In point of fact, he displayed his ignorance to the whole world.

This kind of 'protest' cuts no ice. If an occasion calls for a certain kind of attire, it is considerate to one's host to wear it. One can always be unconventional and off-beat in the privacy of one's own home.

The invitation usually gives a clue as to what one is expected to wear. If the invitation card says 'Decorations', the men are expected to wear white tie and tails, with decorations if they have any. 'White tie' on the invitation card means that you should wear white tie and tails. 'White or black tie' means that most men will wear tails, but a dinner jacket is also acceptable. 'Evening Dress' on the invitation card means that men will wear tails or a dinner jacket, depending on the occasion. 'Black tie' means wear a dinner jacket and 'Dress optional' means wear either a dinner jacket or dark lounge suit.

If the men are wearing tails, the women with them follow suit by wearing their grandest evening gown. Short or long evening dresses go with a dinner jacket and also often accompany a dark lounge suit, although, strictly speaking, this should not be so.

If the invitation gives no clue as to what to wear, the best thing to do is ask your hostess if it is a private party, and others going to it if it is an official function.

Official dances, dinners and evening receptions are usually white tie affairs, but at private dances, it is customary to wear a dinner jacket.

At a cocktail party, a man wears a dark lounge suit, whether the party takes place in the morning or the evening. If you are going on to an evening dress affair afterwards, it is, of course, quite permissible to wear a dinner jacket or tails at a cocktail party.

At a private dinner-party in a servantless house you will wear a dark lounge suit, but some hostesses who still have servants expect their guests to dress for dinner. It is, therefore, safest to ask rather than risk offending your hostess or making yourself conspicuous by being unsuitably attired.

A wedding calls for morning dress.

Full details of correct dress for formal occasions are given in Chapter 2.

A time to come and a time to go

The question of when to arrive would appear to be simple enough, on the surface but, in point of fact, some odd conventions have intervened to complicate this matter.

Cocktail parties: Arrive a little after the time stipulated. On no account should you arrive early.

Dinner and lunch parties: Arrive more or less at the time stated, but, once again, not before.

Formal banquets: If the card stipulates a time for arrival and another one for the meal, for instance, 7.30 for 8.0, arrive somewhere between the two.

Weddings and church ceremonies: The time on the invitation card is the time at which the ceremony begins. You should, therefore, arrive about ten minutes beforehand.

Private dances: If the invitation card says 10 o'clock, people usually start arriving around 10.30 and continue to do so up to midnight.

When to leave can also present a problem, especially if you wish to get away as soon as possible without being rude. At a public dinner you *can* leave before all the speeches have been made, if you absolutely must, but wait at least until a speech has ended. In the case of a preview of some sort, it is perfectly in order to leave after the welcoming speech. But, in any event, never leave during a performance of any sort, whether it be a speech, a song or anything else. Many invitations clearly specify not only the time at which the function will begin, but also when it will end. This makes it perfectly clear when you are expected to make your exit.

With dinner parties, there is no hard and fast rule and you must play it by ear. Most people begin to leave around 11 o'clock. Certainly, it is better to leave a little early than to overstay your welcome. Once you have decided to leave, announce the fact, take leave of your host and hostess and go. Some people say: 'I'm afraid I must be going now,' then continue to sit for another ten minutes, whereupon they again announce their imminent departure. Finally, they get up and linger at the door for another ten minutes or so, finishing first one story, then beginning a new one, brought to mind by the previous one. Meanwhile, the whole room has been distracted by one guest who cannot make up his mind to leave, while the hostess's nerves get more and more frayed.

Once you reach the front door, be off, as it may very well be chilly for your hosts standing there in their indoor clothes.

The art of conversation

Guests have duties as well as privileges and one of their main duties to their hosts is to mingle with the other guests and talk. At the table, you must talk to the person on your left, as well as to the one on your right, except at very small parties, when the conversation will be general.

At strictly business gatherings, it will be mostly shop talk, but we are considering now all the many other social occasions which a businessman has occasion to attend.

The good conversationalist is above all a good listener. He says his piece, then pauses to allow others to say theirs. The man who goes on and on, enamoured of the sound of his own voice and utterly oblivious of anyone else's opinion on the subject, is an ill-mannered bore. A conversation should be an exchange of views, not a soliloquy. A brilliant talker can get away with dominating the conversation and he will not be resented. The trouble is, however, that so many men merely *think* they are brilliant talkers.

Unless it is a dinner for four, it is seldom possible to hold a deep and serious conversation at a social gathering. It is mostly a question of making small talk. The English are supposed to be past-masters at it and it is considered a necessary social accomplishment. Some of the suitable subjects for small talk are topical items such as Wimbledon or Henley in season, a case in the law courts, cars, films and plays with people likely to know about them, books, gardening, even food.

Taboo subjects

In Victorian times, politics, religion, money, sex, and other people were on the list of taboo subjects. Nowadays, sex seems to be the favourite topic of discussion, with no holds barred.

Money is perfectly respectable too, providing you don't go over-
board with: 'How much did you pay for that suit?' Or: 'How
much are they paying you at Scott's?' As for gossip, it is the
mainstay of small talk, providing it is not malicious. It is still

'. . . watch carefully for any sign of the situation getting out of hand'

best to tread a little softly with politics and religion, unless you
do not feel very strongly about either subject. If you do decide
to play with fire and risk either of these two subjects, you should
watch carefully for any sign of the situation getting out of hand.
Risqué stories are still taboo and so are those which expose

others to ridicule. Your operation and illnesses are likewise 'out', however amusingly told. It is rude to talk at length about a person some of the guests do not know.

Incredible as it may seem to many businessmen, there are times when talking shop is definitely taboo. If, for instance, three or four guests are in the same line of business, and the others are not, it is quite wrong for them to discuss the 'state of the market', complete with technical terms which are absolutely meaningless to the other guests. It is equally impolite to discuss business in the presence of women who have absolutely no interest in the subject. If the party is in honour of a consumer who has purchased the millionth car or won a competition or something, then it is quite unthinkable to abandon her in a corner while you proceed to talk shop with some of your fellow executives. Hard as it may seem, it is your duty on such occasions to keep your conversation at the level of the guest of honour, unless, of course, it is a large party, and you can snatch a little surreptitious shop talk here and there!

Asking tactless questions also comes under the heading of taboos, although questions in general can be very useful in drawing shy people into the conversation. Never ask anyone his age, where he went to school or what his father does.

Do not force people to talk about their specialities. Professional people attend parties to relax, not to instruct the layman on the intricacies of their profession. It is very tempting to ask a lawyer about your knotty legal problems and to tell a distinguished physician about your aching back, but it is definitely not done.

Compliments

The young company director felt that he ought to pay a compliment to the gracious lady whom his company was fêting. 'You are good at colours,' he announced emphatically, glaring at her hat, 'your hat matches your dress.'

If you cannot do better than that, it is best for all concerned that you avoid attempting to compliment a lady. Englishmen are singularly inept at paying compliments, and one wonders why.

Perhaps they are afraid of making fools of themselves. But

why should they? All women like receiving compliments, whether they like the man or not. Why then be so parsimonious with a gift so welcome yet costing so little?

An Italian man considers it his duty to pay compliments to a woman and he does it cheerfully, generously, and charmingly. He is certainly not expected to mean what he says to boot.

If, therefore, you can see your way to making a few ladies happy by paying them a gracious compliment, it will help the party to go with a swing. If you feel you *must* be sincere, you will certainly have no great difficulty in finding *something* about the lady you can honestly admire. But with time and practice you will find that the compliment just slips out effortlessly and almost unbidden – in short, it will have become a pleasant habit.

Apologies

If you spill something on the carpet or the tablecloth, or if you break one of your hostess's precious vases, apologize and leave it at that. There is nothing to be gained by going on and on about it. The poor hostess will be sufficiently upset without your forcing her to repeat again and again that it doesn't matter really, it was only a shabby old vase anyway, when in point of fact it was her precious Ming. Don't offer to replace the object – not everything is replaceable and, above all, don't offer to pay for it.

Afterwards you can try to find a reasonably similar object and send it along to her. Otherwise, you can drop her a note of apology and perhaps send her some flowers or chocolates.

Brick-dropping

Some people have a fatal habit of constantly saying the wrong thing at the wrong time to the wrong person, such as the girl who, upon being proudly told by a young man that he was eighteen, replied: 'Are you? I thought you were very much younger.' Thirty years later, the same man would have been delighted by the remark.

Thoughtlessness obviously causes such remarks – not stopping to think what their effect on their audience will be. In other words, a failure to put yourself in the other person's place.

Sometimes an unfelicitous remark has escaped you and you cannot retrieve it. What to do? Some people very bravely follow through, such as the young man, who asked another at a cocktail party: 'Who's the lady over there with spots all over her face?'

'My wife,' the man replied.

'Oh, really?' the young man went on, with apparent unconcern. 'How interesting! Is she the same all over?'

Such aplomb merits applause, but, of course, a wise young man would not have made the original remark. He would have shown a good deal more self-control in his choice of random remarks.

If it is the other person who has made an unfortunate remark at your expense, the kindest thing you can do is let it pass unnoticed. He will be grateful to you and, who knows, one day he may be in a position to return the compliment.

Smoking

At a public dinner the chairman will rise after the last course and propose the loyal toasts. He usually says: 'My Lords, Ladies and Gentlemen, – the Queen.' Everyone rises, raises his glass, says 'The Queen', drinks, and then sits down again.

After this, but not before, smoking is permitted. Sometimes the chairman will announce: 'Gentlemen, you may smoke' – and this goes for the ladies, too. Otherwise, waiters will begin to hand around cigars and cigarettes.

This rule is very stringently followed and no one, however famous or distinguished, can get away with flaunting it. It is, in fact, an excellent rule, as the right time to smoke, if at all, is obviously after a meal.

The barbaric habit of smoking between courses, however many people on either side of the Atlantic may do it, is definitely to be avoided. Even a hostess who herself smokes may well feel slighted if one of her guests spoils not only his own palate, but everyone else's pleasure by mingling the aroma of smoke with that of her carefully-prepared dishes.

When dining in a household you do not visit frequently, the very best procedure is to wait until everyone else is smoking until you yourself do so.

To help or not to help

It is not always easy to decide whether to offer to help your hostess with the clearing up. Some cook-hostesses like a little help, while others definitely prefer to tackle the debris alone when the dust has settled. Sometimes one or two of the women guests help the hostess to clear up afterwards.

This is another of those situations which are best played by ear, depending as they do on the size of the party, the degree of formality of the party, whether or not the hostess has domestic help, and whether she actually wants her guests to give her a hand.

By all means offer to help. If you really mean it and make a move in the right direction, the chances are that your offer will be accepted. If it is not, do not insist. Some people derive genuine pleasure in waiting upon their guests.

After the ball is over

After a formal dinner party you should send your hostess a note of thanks. In fact a 'Thank you' note is always appreciated by a hostess. The most popular guests of all even send a few flowers. After all, preparing a meal for a party, whether small or large, entails a great deal of work and effort, so surely it deserves the courtesy of a short appreciate note in return?

OVERNIGHT VISITS

If invited to spend a week-end in the country or elsewhere, the question of when to arrive will usually be made quite clear to you by your hostess. She will say either: 'The 10.55 train from Euston will get you here in plenty of time for lunch.' Or, if you are driving: 'We shall expect you in time for dinner at eight.'

As for the length of your stay, a 'week-end' is intended to begin with lunch or dinner on Saturday and end after tea on the Sunday. A 'long week-end' means either arriving for dinner on Friday and leaving after tea on Sunday, or arriving for lunch on Saturday and leaving on the Monday, before or after lunch.

Certainly, if your hostess has not made both arrival and departure times perfectly clear, it is up to you to ask. Simply say: 'What time would you like me to arrive?' Of course, you cannot very well say: 'What time would you like to get rid of me?', so time of departure on the long week-end can be a little tricky. The safest bet is to say: 'I'm afraid I'll have to leave fairly early on Monday morning. Is that all right?' Then, if you find your hostess was particularly keen on your staying for lunch, you may be able to let yourself be persuaded to do so.

The thoughtful hostess will give you some indication of what she has planned for your entertainment and you will use this information to guide you as to the clothes you will need to take along. You will normally have very little problem here, as you will usually be invited with golf, shooting, fishing, or some other specific activity in mind. If you have any doubt as to whether they dress for dinner, you can always ask. And certainly you will know in advance if you are to take in a grand ball.

The week-end guest is expected to participate in whatever entertainment the hosts have provided and generally to fit in with the habits of the household. Obviously, you will be punctual for meals, you will ask permission before using the telephone and will turn off lights if you are the last to leave a room.

You will also be as careful of your hosts' possessions as you would of your own and you will leave the bathroom in a fit state for its next occupant.

Your hostess will normally give you your cue with regard to breakfast. She will either announce that breakfast time is such and such or she will ask you whether you would like breakfast in bed. While this may sound too much of a good thing to you, it may very well make things easier for the hostess, so fall in with her wishes if you can.

As for taking care of your own requirements and helping your hostess, this will depend on whether there are servants, occasional help, or no help at all. In the last instance, you will certainly want to inconvenience your hostess as little as possible.

If there *are* servants you will be expected to tip them before you leave. The manservant would expect between 10s and £1, or even 30s if he had been especially attentive. After a hunting week-end, you might tip the groom 10s and leave 15s for the hunt servants. If you have been shooting, the head-keeper will expect anything from £1 a day.

If the servants consist of a couple who live in and do all the work, each guest would tip them 10s for a week-end stay. If there is just a woman who comes in daily and makes your bed and so on, you might leave her 5s or 10s. The cook and the gardener are never tipped and the chauffeur seldom.

If there is no help at all, but you notice that a resident friend or relative is doing rather a lot of housework, it is a thoughtful idea to thank her at the end of your stay and perhaps leave her a small gift, such as a box of chocolates.

This matter of tipping household servants can be quite a delicate one and you can never go wrong in asking your hostess's advice on it.

As for your hostess herself, you will obviously thank her and write her a note as soon as you return home. Strictly speaking, you do not need to thank the host also, but many people prefer to do so.

RESIDENTIAL COURSES

More and more businessmen are attending residential management courses lasting from a single week-end to a week or more and, unquestionably, as the need for professional management grows, the trend will gain momentum.

The schools and colleges providing such courses, whether private or otherwise, vary a great deal in the kind of accommodation and service they can offer their residential students. Some have all the refinements of a first-class hotel, including night porter and 'boots' to clean the residents' shoes, while others offer somewhat more spartan facilities.

Staying at a residential college, therefore, is very much like staying at a hotel, except that there are usually more regulations to be observed. These may concern mealtimes, a time to be back at the college at night, smoking or talking in certain rooms, and

F

so on. Every regulation is made for a definite reason – it is usually a question of staffing – and it is therefore extremely bad manners not to comply.

Naturally, the serving staff do not like to point out to an imposing and important-looking man that breakfast is served only until 8.30 and it is therefore definitely not cricket for the same important-looking man to take advantage of the situation and appear late for breakfast every morning. Good manners demand that you follow the regulations, however irksome they may be.

Having signed on to attend a certain course, good manners also require you to co-operate with the college staff and to participate as requested. Many executives attending management courses have not 'been to school' for ten, twenty, or even more years and the whole exercise seems strange to them. Some of the teaching methods may shock them; others they will think just plain silly. Yet, once present, they must overcome their misgivings and participate in the exercise.

If after participating wholeheartedly and doing the required work you feel at the end of the course that you have gained nothing, you will be fully justified in writing to the college principal and lodging your complaint and you will obviously send none of your subordinates to the college. But passive resistance to the course is inconsiderate both to the teaching staff and to your fellow-participants.

When not actually working, you should mix as much as you possibly can with the others. This is so important that if you should go to the course with one or more other people from your own company, it would pay you to part from them for the duration of the course in favour of talking to as many of the other men as possible.

Half the value of residential courses lies in the exchange of ideas between executives from other companies, other towns, other types of business, other backgrounds. If you spend all your spare time with your own colleagues or some acquaintance you happen to meet at the college, you will not derive full benefit from the course.

As in so many other situations, what you get out of these management courses depends a great deal on what you are willing to put into them.

chapter seven

dealing with the press

Every man in business should strive, if only out of self-interest, to be on good terms with the Press, for the Press can do a tremendous amount for him. It can give free publicity to your company and your products, it can keep you in the news, it can dispose its readers favourably towards your products and your company, it can make it easier for you to find the staff you need. On the other hand, a bad Press can make your company look like a nonentity in the community and present such delicate matters as strikes in an unfavourable light.

With so many facts stacked in favour of dealing fairly and courteously with the Press, it is surprising how many companies in Britain still treat the Press with distrust and suspicion, doing all they can to prevent them from carrying out their news-gathering task.

Ideally, your attitude towards the Press should be one of friendly co-operation, arising from your firm belief in a free Press. If you have a public relations or Press officer, then obviously he or she will make contact with the editor of your local paper, the City editor, and other journalists. Press relations is part of the p.r.o's job and it will be up to him to establish and keep up good Press relations for you and your company. But

Press relations are not something to be delegated and forgotten. You, too, must play your part by granting an interview when asked, by meeting journalists when they call at your plant, by showing appreciation when your product is featured editorially, by giving out as much information as you can rather than drawing a veil of secrecy over everything.

If your company does not have its own public relations department, you should delegate someone as official spokesman for the company in its dealings with the Press. It must be a senior executive, preferably at directorial level, not a junior who does not know what's going on and speaks without authority. The company secretary is a better man for the job than the sales manager, since he is more likely to be at his desk when someone telephones. Indeed, in some small companies whose top executive is fully aware of the importance of Press relations, he himself always deals with the Press.

Whoever this person is, make sure your telephone operator knows. It far too frequently happens that a journalist will call up seeking information and the telephone operator has no idea who to put him through to.

Interviews

If a journalist asks for an interview, it will be to your advantage to grant him one, for if he cannot get the information he seeks from you, he will have to go elsewhere for it and his resultant story may consequently be inaccurate or uncomplimentary to your company. It is a far better policy to see him and tell him the story from your own point of view.

If, on the other hand, you do not want to see him or do not wish to answer his questions over the telephone, then tell him so frankly. Don't try to be a 'smart Alec' and don't give him a lot of hot air. This will only annoy him and make you look foolish.

Assuming you have agreed to the interview, you would do well to prepare yourself ahead of time to answer the journalist's questions. Bear in mind that he is an expert at asking questions and, undoubtedly, he will do his homework and read up something about your industry's background, who your competitors are and so on. If he is a trade-paper journalist he certainly will be well acquainted with your trade. If he is a financial journalist, he will have met literally hundreds of company directors in hundreds of different concerns during the course of a year. You will, therefore, be at something of a disadvantage and it will pay you to prepare yourself ahead of time.

A financial journalist is likely to want some background information on your company, how it has grown, how many shareholders it has, whether they are large or small shareholders and so on. If highly technical matters are involved, you would do well to have the facts typed on a plain sheet of paper and hand it to the reporter so that he can refer to it at leisure.

One thing you can be sure of – whether cub reporter or top-line editor – he will want facts and figures, not waffle. Nothing irritates a journalist more than vague, unsubstantiated claims.

When the journalist arrives, see that the atmosphere is as relaxed and as friendly as possible. Don't fill the room with grim-looking aides who will give the impression that they are there as 'witnesses'.

It has been said that the personality of the man being interviewed has a great deal to do with the way a Press story is written, a friendly personality resulting in a good Press and a cold personality in a bad Press. Obviously, you cannot change your personality in the interests of good Press relations, but it is none the less useful to know which are the qualities present in a likeable personality. Dr William C. Menninger, a distinguished American psychiatrist, enumerates them as follows: (i) sincerity; (ii) personal integrity; (iii) humility; (iv) courtesy; (v) wisdom; and (vi) charity.

During the interview, be as informative and as helpful as you can. A journalist does not expect you to tell him your trade secrets, but welcomes any factual information about your firm which you can give him. While you can expect a trade-paper journalist to be familiar with your industry, a financial journalist might be less so and will, therefore, be eager for some background information on your industry in general and the place of your company in it.

When talking to business magazine journalists about methods you have found to be particularly successful, you would do well to forget about the resultant publicity for your firm and think of it instead as an exercise in sharing your experience with others. Unfortunately, this desire to share with others is very under-developed in British industry, but perhaps one day we, too, will learn what an excellent policy it is.

The question of whether or not to take a journalist on a detailed tour of the factory is an individual one. Certainly you should offer every visiting journalist the opportunity, but you should not insist upon it. Obviously, the trade-paper journalist is likely to be the most eager to tour the plant, although it must be admitted that not all of them are keen to do so. A financial journalist might well be satisfied with a very cursory tour. But it *is* a very individual matter and even some editors of women's glossy magazines are known to enjoy a factory visit and to take a lively interest in what is going on. The best rule, then, is to leave it up to your visitor.

You will certainly want to offer your guest some refreshment, especially if he has travelled a long way to see you. He may not accept, but he will certainly appreciate the offer.

It happens not infrequently that, having granted an interview to a journalist, a businessman is thoroughly dissatisfied with the resultant story in the Press. But it must be realized that the style in which a journalist writes his article and the way in which he treats his subject are entirely his own affair. So is his opinion of your company's shares. He does not presume to tell you how to run your business, so why should you expect to tell him how to do his job? Yet it is incredible how many businessmen try to do just this. The managing director of one manufacturing company once practically demanded that a journalist read back his notes, like a shorthand-typist who had just finished taking dictation.

The only time you have cause for complaint is when a journalist gets his facts wrong or if he misquotes you in such a fashion as to give a completely different meaning to what you said. This *can* happen, of course, since even the best journalists make mistakes. They often work from sketchy notes, frequently have to condense statements to save space, or leave out important qualifying remarks for the same reason, with the result that sometimes you can hardly recognize the story as your own. Luckily, in the majority of cases, no great harm is done, but occasionally a real 'clanger' is dropped and, if you are like most businessmen, you will be furious.

However, unless the misquote is actually libellous, you would be well advised to refrain from sending the editor a scathing letter, since it is most unlikely that he will publish it. It is far more diplomatic to write a letter praising whatever you can find to praise in the article, or the editorial acumen which prompted it, and then go on to say that in the interests of accuracy you wish to correct this or that misstatement. Such a letter stands a very good chance of being published in the correspondence column, since it allows the editor to save face and at the same time to set the record straight which, after all, is the main purpose in having a correction published.

Press parties

The party was going great guns. The Press had turned out *en masse* and people were still crowding around the new models, cocktail glass in hand, when suddenly a mighty voice boomed: 'Everybody out!' It was the managing director's idea of how to bring a Press preview to a graceful conclusion.

This, unfortunately, is not a piece of fiction, even though it illustrates to perfection how *not* to do it.

Frequently, separate previews are given for the Trade Press, the nationals, and the women's magazines, and it *is* sometimes difficult to get one batch of people out in time to prepare for the next arrivals. How not to do it we have already seen. One way to handle the problem is to allow sufficient time between the three events. After that, you can but leave nature to take its course, as it were. It is usually only a few stragglers who hang on and on, and a diplomatic reference to your next arrivals usually takes care of them. If they *still* do not budge, there is nothing for it but to leave them alone and carry on with your plans for the next party. Then it will be they who are bad-mannered and not you.

But let us begin from the beginning.

The kind of event you decide upon has very little, if anything, to do with etiquette. The only point to bear in mind is that the likes and dislikes of your prospective guests must be considered, and not only your own convenience.

As we have seen, the national Press, Trade Press, and women's magazines are really three different worlds inhabited by different kinds of people. The penthouse of a swanky West End hotel suits the girls from the 'glossies' down to the ground, but the more rough and ready Trade magazine men much prefer a Fleet Street public-house, a barrel of beer and some cheese and nuts. It is difficult to please everyone, of course, but it helps at least to know the score.

Quite a number of manufacturers prefer to give very small luncheon parties, inviting a few journalists at a time. In this way they feel they can really buttonhole each guest and sell him on the new line. Most journalists strongly dislike this technique, since it is so wasteful of their time. A journalist likes to go to a preview, get his story, perhaps take a couple of drinks and then get back to the office. He is not so avid as some people seem to think for food and drink. So if you do want to use this approach, organize it in such a way as to take up as little as possible of the guests' time, leaving them free to leave as soon as they want to.

The etiquette connected with sending out the invitations themselves is given in Chapter 9. Address your invitation personally to the news editor, City editor, or to the editor of the magazine in the case of trade, technical, or women's publications. If he cannot attend himself, he will send one of his staff to represent him.

It is useful to realize that while, to you, the launching of a new line of products or new models is an exciting event which only takes place once or twice a year, to a journalist it is an everyday affair. Consequently, your invitation will not seem nearly so exciting to him as it does to you.

If you are keen to get a good attendance, therefore, you will want to do all you can to make sure the top editors attend. One way to attempt this is to write personal letters of invitation to them, on your own personal writing paper, and signed by you, as chief executive of your company. Obviously, the larger your company is, the more successful such a technique is likely to be. Official invitations should follow in the ordinary way and you can mention this in your personal note.

Another thing you can do is telephone your important editors a few days before the preview, saying you hope they will be able to join you. Obviously all of this assumes that you have made it your business to become acquainted with the people in question.

Certainly your public relations officer, or your Press officer, if you have one, will know them and he or she can do much the same.

Since there are so many kinds of Press previews, you should be sure to state specifically on the invitation what kind of a function it is to be, so that the journalist knows what to expect. A journalist's time is very heavily booked, and while he may find the time to go along, get his story and return to the office, he may not be able to spare the time for lunch or for extended film-viewing and so on.

A journalist also likes to know just what he is being asked to go along for. A coy mention of a 'new product', far from arousing his interest, only serves to irritate him. He wants to know what *kind* of a new product. It goes without saying that, unless you have something very specific to show the Press, you should not invite them along at all, since it is not conducive to good Press relations to waste their time.

Anything you can do to help journalists know who's who at the party will be appreciated. It is an excellent idea to have tags giving name and function made out for everyone present. If yours is a sufficiently large organization, it is well worthwhile having different coloured tags for technical people, top management and so on. A journalist often wants to seek out the designers or technical men and knowing who they are helps tremendously.

It is also important to make sure that the technical people are present in the first place. Top-management men often make the mistake of keeping their production, technical, and design people in the background, yet it is precisely these people whom journalists are frequently most anxious to meet.

Top management should also be present, of course. Your public relations department or your consultants will certainly have prepared a Press release about the new products and if they are really on their toes will have placed it, together with photographs and any other relevant material in a Press wallet to be handed to each guest upon arrival. This does not mean, however, that there is nothing left for you to do. If fitting, you will want to say a few words about the new products or other purpose of the preview and then make yourself available to answer questions. Even though your prepared statement is already in their hands, journalists will want to ask questions in an attempt to get an exclusive 'angle' for their paper. It is in your best interests to be as helpful as you can.

Photographs and photographers

Press photographers appreciate courtesy and co-operation every bit as much as the rest of us. Yet they are frequently the victims of bad temper and officiousness at the hands of the very people who have invited them or commissioned them to cover an event. A company chairman or managing director may be eager for publicity for his company and consequently he will invite, or make sure his publicity department invites, a photographer to cover this or that important company function. When the photographer turns up, however, he will not merely fail to co-operate with him so that he can take the shots he needs, but will sometimes even be downright rude to him and act for all the world as if the man were an interloper.

The reason for his boorishness is obvious. He does not wish it to be known that he is eager for publicity or that he wants his photograph taken. But it does seem rather harsh to take it out on the hapless photographer, who is merely trying to do his job to the best of his ability.

People more experienced in such matters and less self-conscious, slip in an unobtrusive aside to the photographers: 'Good afternoon, gentlemen – what do you want me to do?' This enables the photographers to get their shots quickly and with a minimum of disruption and they are then only too happy to get out of the way.

A rather different kind of photographic session takes place when you commission a portrait photographer to take an official photograph of you for general Press use. The public will not be present at the sitting and therefore it should not prove so painful.

It is surprising, none the less, how many executives find the process unpleasant. There really is no reason why it should be. The so-called executive portrait aims to bring out strength and character and the photographer will try to capture these traits. There should also be a hint of good humour and alertness in your expression. You should, therefore, do your best to co-

operate as cheerfully as possible with the photographer and
follow his instructions.

Some photographers specialize in taking photographs of company executives for the Press and they do an excellent and quite

'. . . aims to bring out strength and character'

painless job of it. They usually take four or five different shots,
send you the proofs and from them you select which one is to
be your official portrait. You will then buy the copyright of
your official portrait so that it becomes yours and, subject to your
agreement, any publication can reproduce it free of charge.

chapter eight

order of precedence and forms of address

The information given in this chapter will serve a threefold purpose: it will guide you in your seating arrangements by giving the correct order of precedence; it will show you how to address letters to everyone from Queen to commoner; it will indicate how to address distinguished people verbally, should you have occasion to meet them.

It used to be customary to address the more distinguished of common mortals as Esquire. Later on, it became general to so address almost every man without any other distinguishing title. Now even this practice is falling into disuse and the American one of addressing men as 'Mr' is gradually taking over.

Wives take their husband's name: Mrs John Smith. In business, however, Mrs John Smith will be addressed as Mrs Mary Smith, since no one is expected to know her husband's first name. In fact, the writing is clearly on the wall: the next move will be towards addressing all married women, whether in business or otherwise, by their own Christian name followed by their husband's surname.

Divorcees use their own Christian name and retain their ex-husband's surname, e.g. Mrs Mary Smith, just like the business-woman referred to above. Widows retain their husband's full name, e.g. Mrs John Smith. This is a fairly recent innovation reflecting the widow's desire to differentiate herself from the divorcee.

The widow of a titled person is addressed in the same way as during her husband's life until the successor to the title marries. She then becomes The Dowager Duchess of Blank or The Dowager Lady Brown, as the case may be. Women do not take too kindly to the word Dowager these days and many prefer to use their Christian name, followed by the title, e.g. Elizabeth Lady Brown.

All peers, peeresses, and dowager peeresses below the rank of marquess are entitled to the prefix 'The Rt Hon.' If one such peer is a privy councillor, it is therefore usual to indicate this by putting the initials 'P.C.' after his name. In the case of a commoner who is a privy councillor, the prefix 'The Rt Hon.' is given but the letters 'P.C.' are usually omitted. These letters take precedence over any other initials of status, except K.G., K.T., K.P., V.C., and G.C.

Members of Parliament who are also privy councillors take the letters M.P. after their name, e.g. The Rt Hon. John Brown, M.P. All letters addressed to Members of Parliament should have M.P. after the name. Initials of all Orders precede M.P., e.g. Sir John Brown, K.C.M.G., M.P., Dame Elizabeth Brown, D.B.E., M.P.

Letters denoting membership of learned societies are usually added only if they imply special distinction. You would add F.R.S. (Fellow of the Royal Society), F.B.A. (Fellow of the British Academy), F.S.A. (Fellow of the Society of Antiquaries of London), R.A. (Royal Academician), A.R.A. (Associate of the Royal Academy), but not F.R.Hist.S. (Fellow of the Royal Historical Society), or F.R.G.S. (Fellow of the Royal Geographical Society).

Letters denoting Masters' or Bachelors' degrees, M.A., B.A., B.SC., are rarely used except when writing to someone in the teaching profession.

Other forms of address and order of precedence follow. Bear in mind, however, that the old-fashioned formal way of ending a letter, 'I have the honour to be your obedient servant', etc., is practically never used nowadays, except when writing to a member of the Royal Family. 'Yours faithfully' is commonly used instead. These obsolescent forms are given below more as a reference than a recommendation that they be used.

The Royal Family

THE QUEEN

> *Address on envelope* To Her Majesty the Queen
> *Letter opening* Your Majesty, (or Madam,)
> *Reference in body of letter* Your Majesty
> *Salutation* I have the honour to be, your Majesty's humble and loyal subject,
> *Verbally* Your Majesty. Ma'am (pronounced as written)

THE QUEEN MOTHER

> *Address on envelope* To Her Majesty Queen Elizabeth The Queen Mother
> *Letter opening* Your Majesty, (or Madam,)
> *Reference in body of letter* Your Majesty
> *Salutation* I have the honour to be, your Majesty's humble and loyal subject,
> *Verbally* Your Majesty. Ma'am

PRINCE PHILIP

> *Address on envelope* To His Royal Highness The Prince Philip, Duke of Edinburgh
> *Letter opening* Sir,
> *Reference in body of letter* Your Royal Highness
> *Salutation* I have the honour to be, Sir, your Royal Highness's most humble and obedient servant,
> *Verbally* Your Royal Highness. Sir

PRINCES AND PRINCESSES

> *Address on envelope* To His (or Her) Royal Highness The Prince (or Princess) Blank
> *Reference in body of letter* Your Royal Highness
> *Salutation* I have the honour to be, Sir (or Madam), your Royal Highness's most humble and obedient servant,
> *Verbally* Your Royal Highness. Sir. Ma'am

DUKES AND DUCHESSES OF THE ROYAL BLOOD

> *Address on envelope* To His (or Her) Royal Highness, The Duke (or Duchess) of Blank
> Otherwise as for princes and princesses

Peers and Peeresses

The five classes of peerage, in descending order, are as follows: Duke and Duchess; Marquess and Marchioness; Earl and Countess; Viscount and Viscountess; Baron and Baroness. They are addressed as follows:

DUKE

Address on envelope To His Grace the Duke of Blank
Letter opening My Lord Duke, (less formally: Dear Duke, or Dear Duke of Blank,)
Reference in body of letter Your Grace
Salutation I have the honour to be, My Lord Duke, Your Grace's most devoted and most obedient servant, (less formally: Yours sincerely,)

DUCHESS

Address on envelope To Her Grace the Duchess of Blank
Letter opening Madam, (less formally: Dear Duchess, or Dear Duchess of Blank,)
Reference in body of letter Your Grace
Salutation I have the honour to be, Madam, Your Grace's most humble and most obedient servant, (less formally: Yours sincerely,)

MARQUESS

Address on envelope To The Most Hon. the Marquess of Blank
Letter opening My Lord Marquess, (less formally: Dear Lord Blank,)
Reference in body of letter Your Lordship
Salutation I have the honour to be, my Lord Marquess, Your Lordship's obedient and humble servant, (less formally: Yours sincerely,)

MARCHIONESS

Address on envelope To the Most Hon. the Marchioness of Blank
Otherwise as for a baroness

EARL

Address on envelope To The Right Hon. the Earl (of) Blank
Otherwise as for a baron

COUNTESS

Address on envelope To The Right Hon. the Countess (of) Blank
Otherwise as for a baroness

VISCOUNT

Address on envelope To The Right Hon. the Viscount Blank
Otherwise as for a baron

VISCOUNTESS

Address on envelope To The Right Hon. the Viscountess Blank
Otherwise as for a baroness

BARON

Address on envelope To The Right Hon. the Lord Blank
Letter opening My Lord, or Sir, (less formally: Dear Lord
Blank,)
Reference in body of letter Your Lordship
Salutation I have the honour to be, my Lord, Your Lordship's
obedient and humble servant, (less formally: Yours sincerely,)

BARONESS

Address on envelope To The Right Hon. the Lady Blank
Letter opening Madam, (less formally: Dear Lady Blank,)
Reference in body of letter Your Ladyship
Salutation I have the honour to be, Madam, Your Ladyship's
obedient and humble servant, (less formally: Yours sincerely,)

The titles Baron and Baroness are used only on Court or
parliamentary occasions, although a peeress in her own right is
always called 'Baroness'.

Among acquaintances, peers are known by their Christian
names, but they sign correspondence by their title only, e.g.
'Somerset' alone. Wives use their Christian name in addition,
e.g. 'Mary Somerset'.

The eldest sons of dukes, marquesses, and earls take the highest
of the father's secondary titles, and are addressed according to
that rank. The reason for this abundance of titles is that a dukedom is not usually conferred outright upon a commoner. It is a
question, rather, of working one's way up the ladder over two
or more generations. Having finally achieved a dukedom, the
new duke will retain all his previous titles, conferring the highest
of them upon his heir so that he may spend some time in a lower
rank of the peerage before succeeding to his father's title. The
eldest son's eldest son takes the third title and so on.

Younger sons of dukes and marquesses and all daughters of
dukes, marquesses, and earls take the title 'Lord' or 'Lady' in
addition to their Christian and family names. Daughters of

dukes, marquesses, and earls retain their title after marriage to someone who is not a peer.

The younger sons of earls and all the sons and daughters of viscounts and barons (including life peers) are given the courtesy prefix of 'The Honourable' and this is extended also to their wives. The courtesy title of 'Honourable' is used only on envelopes and in announcements. It is not put on visiting cards and never used in speech. 'Hons.' are referred to as Mr, Mrs, or Miss.

The daughter of a viscount or a baron retains her rank if she marries a commoner. If she marries a Mr Smith, for instance, she becomes The Hon. Mrs Smith. If she marries a man with a title, the prefix 'Honourable' goes before her new title, e.g. Sir James and the Hon. Lady Hardy.

The lowest hereditary title is Baronet, distinguished from Knight by the letters 'Bt' after the name. The wife takes the title 'Lady', followed by the surname, e.g. Lady Jones. The form when writing is as follows:

BARONETS

Address on envelope To Sir John Blank, Bt
Letter opening Sir, (less formally: Dear Sir John,)
Salutation I have the honour to be, Sir, your humble and obedient servant, (less formally: Yours sincerely,)

BARONET'S WIFE

Address on envelope Lady Blank
Letter opening Madam, (less formally: Dear Lady Blank,)
Salutation I have the honour to be, Madam, Your Ladyship's most obedient servant, (less formally: Yours sincerely,)

Decorations and Honours

KNIGHTHOOD

There are ten orders of Knighthood, conferred for distinguished service in any field. The oldest and most distinguished is The Most Noble Order of the Garter. They are listed hereunder in descending order of distinction, with the corresponding initials, which should follow the name of the holder:

G

	Initials
THE MOST NOBLE ORDER OF THE GARTER	K.G.
Conferred on royalty, peers, statesmen	
THE MOST ANCIENT AND MOST NOBLE ORDER OF THE THISTLE	K.T.
Conferred exclusively on distinguished persons of Scottish ancestry	
THE MOST ILLUSTRIOUS ORDER OF ST PATRICK	K.P.
Conferred exclusively on distinguished persons of Irish ancestry	
THE MOST HONOURABLE ORDER OF THE BATH	
Knight Grand Cross	G.C.B.
Knight Commander	K.C.B.
Companion	C.B.

Wives of the first two take the title 'Lady', but wives of the third have no title, only order of precedence.

THE MOST EXALTED ORDER OF THE STAR OF INDIA	
Knight Grand Commander	G.C.S.I.
Knight Commander	K.C.S.I.
Companion	C.S.I.
(no appointments since 1947)	
THE MOST DISTINGUISHED ORDER OF ST MICHAEL AND ST GEORGE	
Knight Grand Cross	G.C.M.G.
Knight or Dame Commander	K.C.M.G., D.C.M.G.
Companion	C.M.G.
THE MOST EMINENT ORDER OF THE INDIAN EMPIRE	
Knight Grand Commander	K.G.C.I.E.
Knight Commander	K.C.I.E.
Companion	K.I.C.
(no appointments since 1947)	
THE ROYAL VICTORIAN ORDER	
Conferred for personal services to the Sovereign. There are five classes, the first two having the title of Knight or Dame:	
Knight or Dame Grand Cross	G.C.V.O.
Knight or Dame Commander	K.C.V.O., D.C.V.O.
Commander	C.V.O
Member Fourth Class	M.V.O.
Member Fifth Class	M.V.O.
THE MOST EXCELLENT ORDER OF THE BRITISH EMPIRE	
There are five classes, for both men and women:	
Knight or Dame Grand Cross	G.B.E.

	Initials
Knight or Dame Commander	K.B.E., D.B.E.
Commander	C.B.E.
Officer	O.B.E.
Member	M.B.E.

KNIGHT BACHELOR, takes no initials

In correspondence, knights are addressed in the same style as baronets, but with the letters of the appropriate Order of Chivalry after their name instead of Bt. Wives of knights take the title Lady followed by the husband's surname. Dames are addressed as Dame Mary Brown, followed by the initials of the appropriate Order.

In addressing a knight holding more than one degree in one or more Orders of Chivalry, show only the senior appointment in each order, e.g., G.C.V.O. and not G.C.V.O., K.C.V.O., M.V.O.

OTHER ORDERS   *Initials*

VICTORIA CROSS

    The most distinguished decoration, awarded for conspicuous bravery in the face of the enemy to all branches of the Armed Forces. It could be conferred on women, but none has been so far.   V.C.

ORDER OF MERIT

    Limited to 24 members   O.M.

ORDER OF THE COMPANIONS OF HONOUR

    For both men and women   C.H.

THE ROYAL ORDER OF VICTORIA AND ALBERT

    For women only   V.A.
    (No appointment since death of Queen Victoria)

THE IMPERIAL ORDER OF THE CROWN OF INDIA

    For women only   C.I.
    (No appointments since 1947)

ROYAL RED CROSS

    For women only   R.R.C.

Honours initials should never appear on visiting cards, but may be given on the envelope. Initials indicating professional qualifications or official status should be used only for professional or official correspondence. Exceptions are Q.C. (Queen's Counsel) and M.P. (Member of Parliament), which are used in all correspondence. Decorations take precedence over degrees. The order of decorations is as follows: V.C., G.C., K.G., K.T., K.P., P.C., G.C.B., O.M., G.C.S.I., G.C.M.G., G.C.I.E., V.A., C.I., G.C.V.O., G.B.E., C.H., K.C.B.,

K.C.S.I., K.C.M.G., K.C.I.E., K.C.V.O., K.B.E., C.B., C.S.I., C.M.G., C.I.E., C.V.O., C.B.E., D.S.O., M.V.O. (Fourth Class), O.B.E., I.S.O., M.V.O. (Fifth class), M.B.E., R.R.C. (First class), D.S.O., M.C., D.F.C., A.F.C., R.R.C. (Second class), A.M., D.C.M., C.G.M., G.M., D.S.M., M.M., D.F.M., A.F.M., B.E.M., V.D., T.D., E.D.

Religious Denominations

CHURCH OF ENGLAND

In descending order, the ranks are: Archbishop, Bishop, Suffragan Bishop, Dean, Provost, Archdeacon, Canon, Prebendary, Rector, Vicar, Curate, or Minister. They are addressed as follows:

ARCHBISHOP

Address on envelope To His Grace the Lord Archbishop of Blank
Letter opening My Lord Archbishop, (less formally: Dear Archbishop, or Dear Archbishop of Blank,)
Reference in body of letter Your Grace
Salutation I remain, my Lord Archbishop, your Grace's most devoted and obedient servant, (less formally: Yours sincerely,)
Verbally Your Grace

When retired, archbishops are referred to by their name, e.g. Archbishop Blank. Envelopes are addressed: The Most Reverend John Blank.

BISHOP AND SUFFRAGAN BISHOP

Address on envelope The Right Rev. the Lord Bishop of Blank
Letter opening My Lord Bishop, (less formally: Dear Bishop, or Dear Bishop of Blank,)
Reference in body of letter Your Lordship
Salutation I am, my Lord, your most obedient servant, (less formally: Yours sincerely,)

DEAN

Address on envelope To The Very Rev. the Dean of Blank
Letter opening Very Reverend Sir, (less formally: Dear Dean,)
Salutation I have the honour to be, Very Reverend Sir, your most obedient servant, (less formally: Yours sincerely,)

PROVOST

Address on envelope The Very Rev. The Provost of Blank

Letter opening Very Reverend Sir, (less formally: Dear Mr Provost, or Dear Provost,)
Salutation I have the honour to be, Very Reverend Sir, your most obedient servant, (less formally: Yours sincerely,)

ARCHDEACON

Address on envelope To The Venerable The Archdeacon of Blank
Letter opening Venerable (or Reverend) Sir, (less formally: Dear Archdeacon,)
Salutation I remain, Venerable (or Reverend) Sir, yours obediently, (less formally: Yours sincerely,)

CANON

Address on envelope The Rev. Canon Brown
Letter opening Reverend Sir, (less formally: Dear Canon, or Dear Canon Brown,)
Salutation I have the honour to be, Reverend Sir, your obedient servant, (less formally: Yours sincerely,)

PREBENDARY

As for Canon

RECTOR, VICAR, CURATE OR MINISTER

Address on envelope To The Rev. John Blank
In the case of a clergyman possessing a title, the clerical rank comes first, e.g. The Reverend the Honourable C. J. Brown
Letter opening Reverend Sir (less formally: Dear Mr Smith,)
Salutation I am, Reverend Sir, your obedient servant, (less formally: Yours sincerely,)

ROMAN CATHOLIC

The order of precedence in the Roman Catholic Church is as follows: The Pope, Cardinal, Archbishop, Bishop, Canon, Monsignor, Abbot, Provincial, Dom, and Priest. Within the Roman Catholic community, the form of address is as follows:

THE POPE

Address on envelope His Holiness Pope Paul VI
Letter opening Your Holiness, or Most Holy Father,
Reference in body of letter Your Holiness
Salutation I have the honour to remain, Your Holiness's most devoted and obedient child, or Your Holiness's most humble child

CARDINAL

Address on envelope To His Eminence Cardinal Blank, Archbishop of——,
(if he is also an Archbishop)
Letter opening My Lord Cardinal, or My Lord, (less formally: Dear Cardinal, or Dear Cardinal Blank,)
Reference in body of letter Your Eminence
Salutation I have the honour to remain, my Lord Cardinal, (or My Lord,) your Eminence's devoted and obedient child, (less formally: Yours sincerely,)
Verbally Your Eminence

ARCHBISHOP

Address on envelope The Most Rev. James Smith, Archbishop of Blank, or His Grace The Archbishop of Blank
Letter opening My Lord Archbishop, (less formally: Dear Archbishop, or Dear Archbishop of Blank,)
Reference in body of letter Your Grace
Salutation I have the honour to remain, my Lord Archbishop, Your Grace's devoted and obedient child, (less formally: Yours sincerely,)
Verbally Your Grace

The official form within the British Commonwealth is as follows:

Address on envelope The Most Rev. Archbishop Brown
Letter opening Most Reverend Sir,
Salutation I have the honour to be your faithful servant,

BISHOP

Address on envelope The Right Rev. The Lord Bishop of Blank or The Rt Rev. James Smith, Bishop of Blank
Letter opening My Lord, or My Lord Bishop, (less formally: Dear Bishop,)
Salutation I have the honour to remain, Your Lordship's obedient child (or servant) (less formally: Yours sincerely,)
Verbally Your Lordship

For Irish Bishops, use the same form, except on envelopes, which should be addressed: The Most Rev. The Bishop of Blank

CANON

Address on envelope The Very Rev. Canon Blank
Letter opening Very Rev. Sir, (less formally: Dear Canon Blank,)
Salutation I have the honour to remain, Very Rev. Sir, your

obedient servant, (less formally: Yours sincerely,)
Verbally Canon Blank

MONSIGNOR

Address on envelope The Right (or Very) Rev. Monsignor
Blank or The Right (or Very) Rev. Monsignore
Letter opening Very Rev. Sir, (less formally: Dear Monsignore,)
Salutation I have the honour to remain, Right Rev. Sir, your
devoted and obedient servant, (less formally: Yours sincerely,)
Verbally Monsignor or Monsignore

ABBOT

Address on envelope The Right Rev. The Abbot of Blank
Letter opening My Lord Abbot, or Right Rev. Abbot, or Right
Rev. Father, (less formally: My dear Father Abbot,)
Salutation I beg to remain, My Lord Abbot (or other form
used), your devoted and obedient servant, (less formally: Yours
sincerely,)
Verbally Father Abbot

PROVINCIAL

Address on envelope The Very Rev. Father Blank or The Very
Rev. Father Provincial (followed by the distinguishing initials
of his order)
Letter opening Very Rev. Father, (less formally: My dear
Father,)
Salutation I beg to remain, Very Rev. Father, your devoted and
obedient child, (less formally: Yours sincerely,)
Verbally Father Blank

DOM

Address on envelope The Rev. Dom W. Brown, O.S.B.
Letter opening Dear Rev. Father, (less formally: Dear Dom
William Brown,)
Verbally Father

PRIEST

Address on envelope The Rev. Father Smith
Letter opening Dear Rev. Father, (less formally: Dear Father,)
Verbally Father

JEWISH

CHIEF RABBI

Address on envelope The Very Rev. Chief Rabbi A. Cohen
Letter opening Very Rev. and dear Sir, (less formally: Dear
Chief Rabbi Cohen,)

Salutation I am, Very Rev. and dear Sir, your obedient servant, (less formally: Yours sincerely,)
Verbally Chief Rabbi Cohen

RABBI

Address on envelope The Rev. Rabbi A. Cohen
Letter opening Rev. and dear Sir, your obedient servant, (less formally: Dear Rabbi Cohen,)
Salutation I am, Rev. and dear Sir, (less formally: Yours sincerely,)
Verbally Rabbi Cohen

MINISTER

Address on envelope The Rev. A. Cohen, or The Rev. Dr A. Cohen, according to the case
Letter opening Rev. and dear Sir, (less formally: Dear Mr (or Dr) Cohen,)
Salutation I am, Rev. and dear Sir, your obedient servant, (less formally: Yours sincerely,)
Verbally Mr Cohen or Dr Cohen, according to the case

The Armed Services

When men are of equal rank, order of precedence is in seniority of the service: Navy first, Army second, Royal Air Force third.
Ranks descend in the following order:

Navy	Army	Air Force
Admiral of the Fleet	Field Marshal	Marshal of the Royal Air Force
Admiral	General	Air Chief Marshal
Vice-Admiral	Lieutenant-General	Air Marshal
Rear-Admiral	Major-General	Air Vice-Marshal
Commodore	Brigadier	Air Commodore
Captain	Colonel	Group Captain
Commander	Lieutenant-Colonel	Wing Commander
Lieutenant-Commander	Major	Squadron Leader
Lieutenant	Captain	Flight Lieutenant
Sub-Lieutenant	Lieutenant or Ensign in Brigade of Guards	Flying Officer
	Cornet in Household Cavalry	
	Second Lieutenant or Ensign in Brigade of Guards	Pilot Officer

WOMEN'S SERVICES

W.R.N.S.	*W.R.A.C.*	*W.R.A.F.*
Director	Brigadier	Air Commandant
Superintendent	Colonel	Group Officer
Chief Officer	Lieutenant-Colonel	Wing Officer
First Officer	Major	Squadron Officer
Second Officer	Captain	Flight Officer
Third Officer	Lieutenant	Section Officer
	Second Lieutenant	Assistant Section Officer

Members of the Armed Services are addressed as follows:

COMMISSIONED RANKS

Address on envelope According to rank. Include either the full Christian name or initials of the addressee. e.g. Lieutenant-General A. B. Mostyn; Air Commodore C. D. Lewis, R.A.F., Group Officer B. S. Richards, W.R.A.F.

If an officer is titled, the Service rank is given first, e.g. Admiral Sir George Cunningham, Squadron Leader The Hon F. V. James

Sub-Lieutenants, Midshipmen and Cadets in the Royal Navy, Lieutenants and Second-Lieutenants in the Army, and Flying Officers and Pilot Officers in the Royal Air Force are referred to as 'Mr' and therefore their letters should be addressed Esq., followed by R.N., the name of their regiment, or R.A.F. respectively for each of the Services, e.g. F. Brown, Esq., R.N., J. J. Jackson, Esq., Coldstream Guards, M. W. Jones, Esq., R.A.F.

Decorations should be given after the name, e.g. Captain E. H. Marshall, D.S.O., R.N.

The holder of a subsidiary rank is usually addressed in personal letters by the next rank higher up, e.g. Vice-Admirals and Rear-Admirals would both be addressed as Admiral; Lieutenant-Generals and Major-Generals would both be addressed as General. The envelope is, of course, addressed with their proper rank.

Letter opening Sir or Madam, (less formally: Dear Major Smith,). Chaplains should be addressed both in writing and in speech according to their rank as clergymen. On envelopes, the name is followed by the letters C.F., meaning Chaplain to the Forces.

Letters to the chief chaplains may be addressed to:
Royal Navy: Chaplain of the Fleet
Army: Chaplain-General of the Forces
Royal Air Force: Chaplain-in-Chief

OTHER RANKS

Address on envelope Letters to all other ranks are usually addressed with the number and rank preceding the surname, which is followed by the initials of the addressee, e.g. 196524 A. B. Freeman, D.W.; 986432 A. C. Copland, K.R. The following is also correct usage: 165795 Private J. W. Atkins, R.E.; W/12345 Private H. P. Swift, W.R.A.F.

Civic dignitaries

LORD MAYOR

The Lord Mayors of London, York, Belfast, Dublin, Cardiff, Sydney, Melbourne, Adelaide, Brisbane, and Hobart alone have the privilege of being styled 'Right Hon.'
Address on envelope To The Right Hon. the Lord Mayor of Blank, or To The Lord Mayor of Blank, otherwise as for a baron.

The other cities which have a Lord Mayor are: Birmingham, Bradford, Bristol, Coventry, Hull, Leeds, Leicester, Liverpool, Manchester, Newcastle, Norwich, Nottingham, Plymouth, Portsmouth, Sheffield, Stoke-on-Trent. In these cases address the envelope as follows: To The Right Worshipful The Lord Mayor of Blank (or Lady Mayoress of Blank).

In Scotland, the equivalent status of a Lord Mayor is Lord Provost. The Lord Provost of Aberdeen, Dundee, Edinburgh, Elgin, Glasgow, and Perth are addressed as 'My Lord' and envelopes should read: The Lord Provost of Blank.

LADY MAYORESS

The wife of a Lord Mayor (Lady Mayoress) is styled the same as her husband, but only during his term of mayoralty.

MAYOR

Address on envelope (if of a city) To The Right Worshipful The Mayor of Blank; (if of a borough) To The Worshipful The Mayor of Blank
Letter opening Sir, (or Madam,) (less formally: Dear Mr Mayor, or Dear Mr Brown, Dear Madam Mayor,)
Salutation I am, your Worship's most obedient servant, (less formally: Yours sincerely,)
Verbally Your Worship (on the bench or on public occasions), Mr Mayor (in conversation)

PROVOST

Address on envelope The Provost of Blank
Letter opening Sir,

SHERIFF

Address on envelope The Sheriff of Blank
Letter opening Sir,
Verbally My Lord (in court) or Sheriff

RECORDER AND J.P.

Address on envelope John Brown, Esq., J.P.
Letter opening Dear Sir,
Verbally Your Worship (in court only)

ALDERMAN

Address on envelope Alderman John Brown or (if titled) Alderman Sir John Brown
Letter opening Dear Mr (or Mrs) Alderman Brown or Dear Sir John, (according to case)
Verbally Your Worship (on the bench), Mr (or Mrs) Alderman (in conversation)

BAILIE

Address on envelope Bailie George White or Bailie Sir George White (according to the case)
Letter opening Dear Sir,
Verbally Your Worship (on the bench) Bailie (in conversation)

The Law

THE LORD CHANCELLOR

Address on envelope To The Right Hon. the Lord High Chancellor
Letter opening My Lord, (less formally: Dear Lord Blank,)
Reference in body of letter Your Lordship
Salutation I have the honour to remain your Lordship's obedient servant, (less formally: Yours sincerely,)
Verbally Sir or My Lord

LORD CHIEF JUSTICE

Address on envelope To The Right Hon. The Lord Chief Justice of England or (according to rank) To The Right Hon. Lord Blank, Lord Chief Justice of England
Letter opening My Lord, (less formally: Dear Lord Blank,)

Reference in body of letter Your Lordship
Salutation I remain, my Lord, your obedient servant, (less formally: Yours sincerely,)
Verbally Sir or My Lord

SOLICITOR-GENERAL

Address on envelope To The Right Hon. Sir John Blank, Solicitor-General, Q.C.
Letter opening Sir, (less formally: Dear Sir John,)
Salutation I remain, Sir, yours truly, (less formally: Yours sincerely,)
Verbally Sir

JUDGE OF THE HIGH COURT OF JUSTICE IN ENGLAND, CHANCERY AND OTHER DIVISIONS

Address on envelope To The Hon. Mr Justice Brown, or (if a Knight) To The Hon. Sir John Brown
Letter opening My Lord, or Sir, (less formally: Dear Mr Brown, or Dear Sir John,)
Reference in body of letter Your Lordship
Salutation I have the honour to be, my Lord (or Sir) your obedient servant, (less formally. Yours sincerely,)
Verbally My Lord or Your Lordship when on bench. Sir (in conversation)

JUDGE OF COUNTY COURT

Address on envelope His Honour Judge Smith
Otherwise as for a High Court Judge

JUDGE OF THE COURT OF SESSIONS IN SCOTLAND

Address on envelope To The Hon. Lord Blank
Letter opening My Lord, (less formally: Dear Lord Blank,)
Salutation I have the honour to be, my Lord, your Lordship's obedient servant, (less formally: Yours sincerely,)
Verbally My Lord (when on bench), Sir (in conversation)

WIFE OF A JUDGE OF THE COURT OF SESSIONS IN SCOTLAND

Address on envelope Lady Blank
Letter opening Madam, (less formally: Dear Lady Blank,)
Salutation I have the honour to be, Madam, your Ladyship's obedient servant, (less formally: Yours sincerely,)

The Diplomatic Service

BRITISH AMBASSADOR ABROAD
> *Address on envelope* To His Excellency Her Britannic Majesty's
> Ambassador Extraordinary and Plenipotentiary ——
> *Letter opening* Sir, (or according to rank), (less formally: Dear
> Sir John, or as the case may be)
> *Reference in body of letter* Your Excellency
> *Salutation* I have the honour to be, Sir, your Excellency's most
> humble and obedient servant, (less formally: Yours sincerely,)

FOREIGN AMBASSADOR TO THE COURT OF ST JAMES
> *Address on envelope* To His Excellency the Ambassador Extra-
> ordinary and Plenipotentiary of ——
> *Letter opening* Sir, (or according to rank)
> *Salutation* I have the honour to be, Sir, Your Excellency's most
> humble and obedient servant.

CONSUL
> *Address on envelope* G. J. Brown, Esq., Consul of Her Britannic
> Majesty at ——
> *Letter opening* Sir, (or according to rank) (less formally: Dear
> Mr Brown, or according to rank)
> *Salutation* Yours faithfully,

The medical profession

SURGEON
> *Address on envelope* M. W. Stoddard, Esq., F.R.C.S. (or other
> degree letters)
> *Letter opening* Sir, (less formally: Dear Mr Stoddard,)
> *Salutation* Yours faithfully, (less formally: Yours sincerely,)

PHYSICIAN AND GENERAL PRACTITIONER
> *Address on envelope* Dr F. J. Winter or F. J. Winter, Esq., M.D.
> (or other degree letters)
> *Letter opening* Sir, (less formally: Dear Dr Winter,)
> *Salutation* Yours faithfully, (less formally: Yours sincerely,)

chapter nine

visiting and invitation cards

Visiting cards

Your visiting card, whether business, professional or personal, is your herald going before you to announce your imminent arrival, or bearing some other message from you. Quite frequently, a stranger will see first your card and then you. It is, therefore, very important for your cards to be correct in every detail so that they may create a favourable image of your company and of yourself. It is impossible to create a first-rate impression with second-rate materials.

The enlightened top executive follows this reasoning for everyone in his company, for it is not merely false economy but also poor judgment for a managing director to have elegant engraved cards for himself and cheap printed ones for his sales representatives.

The best way to make sure your cards are right is to take the advice of a reputable stationer, not, however, the small printer around the corner or any stationer on the high street, for there are many cards offered for sale which are quite incorrect, however cheerful or engaging they may be.

All visiting cards should be engraved on good quality card. This requirement is common to business, professional, and personal cards. Otherwise the three vary slightly.

Business cards: Considerable latitude is allowed both with regard to size and to layout. More information has to go on it and therefore it is usually larger than a professional card. Top executives often have their name in the middle and the firm's name underneath. Business cards for sales representatives usually have the name of the company in the middle, the address in the bottom left-hand corner, telephone number in the top left-hand corner, and the representative's name in the bottom right-hand corner. There are no hard and fast rules, however, and any practical layout is quite acceptable. 'Mr' is optional in business cards. Most businessmen seem to prefer to leave it out. It is perfectly in order to include personal qualifications, orders, degrees, and decorations.

Professional cards: These should measure 3 in. × 1¾ in. The name is in the middle and is followed by professional degrees in the case of doctors, dentists, accountants, and so on. Lawyers leave out the degrees, but may add the words barrister-at-law or solicitor. The address goes in the bottom left-hand corner and the telephone number on the right.

Business and professional cards should be used only for business purposes.

Personal cards: Fractionally smaller than professional cards, they should be 3 in. × 1½ in. for men and either 3 in. × 2 in. or 3⅝ in. × 2⅜ in. for women. Joint cards for husband and wife should be 3⅝ in. × 2⅜ in. The name should be prefixed by Mr, Mrs, Miss, or Mr and Mrs, or the appropriate title, according to the case. The prefix 'Hon.' is never used on a visiting card, neither are personal qualifications, orders, degrees, and decorations. The name goes in the centre of the card, the address in the bottom left-hand corner, and the telephone number in the bottom right-hand corner.

Black borders, following bereavements, are no longer used on cards or letters.

The elaborate ritual of card-leaving and calling is now happily

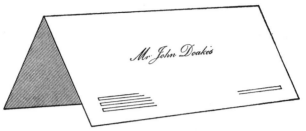

Fig. 3. The informal card

a thing of the past, although it is still practised to a certain extent in some circles. Personal visiting cards have, therefore, lost their original use and are used instead to accompany a gift of flowers, to scribble a hasty note, to convey an address, and so on. Since most of these new uses call for more room than a visiting card affords, the need has arisen for a larger card and this need has been filled by that American invention, the 'informal'. It is a sort of double visiting card, folded at the top, with a blank page behind (see Fig. 3). These are extremely practical and can be printed from the same engraved plate as the cards.

Invitation cards

When it comes to invitation cards, the rule about engraving has been relaxed, largely because of the very high cost involved. It is now considered perfectly correct for both companies and individuals to use printed invitation cards. However, it is as well to bear in mind that invitations to the most fashionable weddings, to elaborate dinner parties and dances, many cocktail parties, and a number of business functions are still engraved. If your company markets a luxury product, or if your business is *haute couture*, perfumery, a first-class hotel, or anything else which depends on an image of costliness and exclusiveness, then you will certainly want to consider engraved invitation cards for your functions.

The lettering on engraved cards should be copperplate. On printed cards it should be letterpress script. The lettering should be black, never silver or coloured, and the paper should be white, of good quality and weight. The cheerful cards on sale at most stationers, with deckle edges, and cocktail glasses, horse-shoes, and what-have-you for decoration are considered to be in bad taste. The plain, spartan, engraved card is supposed to be in the very best of good taste. The man who can afford to make up his own mind pleases himself.

The day and month of the function should be given, but not the year, e.g. Saturday, June 3rd is sufficient. O'clock is considered preferable to a.m. or p.m. Some people even like to quibble about whether R.S.V.P. should go in the bottom right-hand corner or in the opposite one. In point of fact, it is best to let common-sense settle this minor detail and put it on the right if there is sufficient room and on the left if this results in a more balanced layout.

Guests' names should be written in on the invitation cards by hand. Guests should be addressed as Mr John Smith, Miss Mary Brown, Mr and Mrs Warren, Lord and Lady Blank and so on, according to case. The prefix 'Hon.' or letters after names are never used on invitation cards. A doctor and his wife are addressed as Dr and Mrs A. B. White. When a man has both a service rank and a title, usually only the title is used on the card. Admiral Sir Arthur and Lady Winslow would be addressed as Sir Arthur and Lady Winslow. A great many invitations to business functions do not give the guests' names at all, but an engraved card simply 'requests the pleasure of your company' to whatever the function may be.

Socially, the 'At Home' card is used for invitations to cocktail parties, informal dinners and dances and almost any other kind of reception, except, of course, weddings. 'At Home' cards can be engraved with the hostess's name, 'At Home', R.S.V.P. and the address, while the other details are filled in by hand. Such a card, when filled in, would look like Fig. 4.

Equally acceptable and less expensive are cards with only 'At Home', 'Cocktails', and R.S.V.P. printed or engraved on them. Before they are filled in, these cards, which can be bought from any stationer, look like Fig. 5.

For formal dinners, dances, and other functions specially printed or engraved cards can be bought from a stationer or specially ordered. As with 'At Home' cards, the ready-printed cards need to have the names of host or hostess, as well as the address and details of the party, filled in by hand. If a special

H

Mr and Mrs John Brown

Mrs Robert Blake

At Home

Wednesday June 10th

R.S.V.P.
23 Merrivale,
London, S.W.3

Cocktails
6 o'clock

Fig. 4. An 'At Home' card

. . . .

At Home

. . . .

R.S.V.P.   Cocktails

Fig. 5. A more simple 'At Home' card

card is being printed or engraved, it would look like Fig. 6 (overleaf), when properly filled in.

The trend among young people today is to omit the Mr and Mrs both before the host and hostess's name and before the name of the guests. This gives us John and Mary Brown inviting Michael and Carole White.

These invitation cards, printed or engraved specifically for a particular function, bring us closer to the kind of invitation which every company sends out from time to time. All the points previously mentioned are equally valid for company-sent invitations. The main difference is that there is seldom a host and hostess at company functions, so that invitations are sent out in a number of different ways. Some companies send them out in the name of the company alone, e.g.

Wentworth's

The Clothiers

request the pleasure of the company of

Other companies send out invitations in the name of their directors, as follows:

The Directors

of

Snogo Company Limited

Sometimes invitations are sent in the name of the chairman and directors, at other times the chairman's name or that of another top man is given. Each of these forms is correct and the choice is entirely up to you, if it is your party.

As already mentioned, company invitations do not always have each guest's name written in. An example of one such case is shown in Fig. 7 overleaf.

Mr and Mrs John Brown
request the pleasure of

Mr and Mrs Michael White's

company at dinner on

Wednesday, November 10th at 8 o'clock

The Gables,
Crooked Lane,
Gerrards Cross,
Buckinghamshire,   *R.S.V.P.*

Fig. 6. An example of a ready-printed invitation card

Marley's of London
Perfumers

request the pleasure of your company

on the occasion of the launching of their new fragrance

Starry Night

on May 10th

R.S.V.P.
10 Old Bond Street,
London, W.1   *6 to 8 o'clock*

Fig. 7. An example of a company invitation card

Business functions are frequently held at hotels or other premises removed from the place of business. Replies, however, are wanted at the office and perhaps the managing director's secretary is in charge of collecting them. In such cases the invitations may read as in Fig. 8.

The Directors of
Snogo Company Limited
request the pleasure of the company of

Mr John Myers

at a buffet luncheon to be held at the
Hyde Park Hotel, Knightsbridge,
London, S.W.1
on Tuesday, October 30th
between 12.30 and 2 o'clock

R.S.V.P.
Miss P. Evans,
12 Bruton Street,
London, S.W.3

Fig. 8. Another company invitation card

Business invitations should be sent to a person's business address. Purely social invitations should be sent to the home address.

Replying to formal invitations

A business invitation should be replied to on the firm's letter-head. An invitation sent to your home address should be replied to on your own personal writing paper.

Some invitations simply cannot be turned down, unless you are actually under sedatives. Invitations by Royalty or to meet Royalty come under this heading, as well as some invitations from your superiors. It is usually possible, however, to get out of a few of the latter, providing you have a really plausible-sounding excuse but, on the whole, if the boss invites you to dinner, it will pay you to go.

If you do have to turn down an invitation, it is only polite to give the reason, e.g. absence abroad, illness, previous engagement, and so on. Your reply should be in the same tenor as the invitation, that is, in the third person, addressed to the company or person named on the invitation and calling yourself Mr John Brown or plain John Brown, as the invitation was written. This makes answering invitations eminently easy – you simply follow suit, as it were. This, for instance, is Mr John Myers turning down his invitation from Snogo:

> Mr John Myers thanks the Directors
> of Snogo Company Limited for their
> kind invitation to the buffet luncheon
> on October 30, and regrets that he
> is unable to attend owing to a previous
> engagement.

It will be typed on his firm's letterhead, in the middle of the page.

When accepting an invitation, you repeat the time and venue of the function to indicate you have duly noted them. Here is how one of Marley's anonymous guests would have replied:

> Mr Thomas White thanks Marley's of London
> for their kind invitation for May 10, at 6 to
> 8 o'clock and has pleasure in accepting.

Since Marley's did not mention anything more specific than the launching of their new fragrance, there is no point in repeating the whole thing in the acceptance.

Send in your reply as soon as possible, to enable the organizers to estimate the number of guests to expect. Very many business-men do not bother to answer invitations at all. They simply turn up if it suits them and toss the card in the waste-paper basket if it does not. Needless to say, this is exceedingly rude. R.S.V.P means answer, if you please. Could anyone ask more politely?

chapter ten

letter-writing

Like most other businessmen, you probably spend a part of every day dictating letters. These letters either help to create goodwill for you and your company, or else they irritate and antagonize their recipients, depending on how they are written.

A friendly, unhackneyed, diplomatic letter can help you to sell your products, placate an irate customer, and generally influence its recipient in your favour, quite apart from making most business transactions smoother and pleasanter for everyone concerned.

It is, therefore, well worthwhile taking the trouble to master the art of letter-writing and also to make sure that all members of the staff who come under your jurisdiction are well versed in the art. The policy of delegating the firm's letter-writing to a soulless scribe reared on the 'commercialese' of bygone days is a very poor one.

Stationery

Etiquette does not come into the preparation of a business letter-head. It used to be *de rigueur* to have it engraved, but nowadays

it is quite permissible to have it printed instead. It will pay you
to have the layout prepared by a competent firm, well versed in
the most up-to-date typefaces. And if you want to project the
image of quality, you will also need to select a good bond paper.
Inevitably, a cheap, old-fashioned letter-head cannot impress its
viewers as coming from an up-to-date company selling quality
merchandise.

On the other hand, a company marketing antiques or otherwise wishing to create an aura of old-world dignity would do
better to select one of the older typefaces, a conventional layout
and have the letter-heads die-stamped on good quality paper.

It is not good form to write personal letters on business
stationery. It is better to keep a supply of your personal writing
paper handy at the office. However, this is not an endorsement of
private letter-writing in the office.

Personal writing paper should be engraved, not printed. Your
address can go either in the centre, at the top of the page, or
indented, in the right-hand top corner, with the telephone number across the opposite corner. Use a simple typeface. Upper-case
throughout is more usual than upper- and lower-case.

The most popular size for personal writing paper is 8 in. × 6 in.
and certainly a man would not want to select anything smaller.
You will want to have a good quality paper and if you do not
know paper, you would do well to seek the advice of a good
stationer. As for colour, it is entirely a question of taste, although
white or grey seems an excellent idea for a man. Some people
consider deckle edges and coloured borders to be in bad taste,
but there are those who refuse to be bound by such arbitrary
rules.

Peers frequently have a coronet engraved both on the paper
and the flap of the envelope, while some people use their family
crest in this way. Nowadays this latter custom is considered a
trifle pretentious, but it enjoyed a great vogue in Victorian times,
when stationers cheerfully suggested a crest to their customers,
regardless of whether it actually belonged to that particular
family or not.

A lot of nonsense used to be written about certain shapes of
envelopes being in better taste than others and about some types
of flap being 'unacceptable', but such snobbery is now very much
a thing of the past. The far more important considerations of

practicability have now taken over and the Postmaster General recommends that from July 1968 envelopes be no smaller than 5½ in. × 3½ in. and no larger than 9¼ in. × 4¾ in. Envelopes between these sizes should have the longer side 1·414 times the

'. . . whether it actually belonged to that particular family or not'

length of the shorter side. Envelopes which do not conform to the Post Office preferred sizes will be charged at the next highest rate. These recommended sizes will enable the Post Office to use new automatic and electronic sorting equipment, aimed at keeping down the cost of the postal service. The Postmaster General makes no mention of flaps which are too pointed!

The art of writing

Writing is both a natural gift and a craft. If you were not born with the gift, no one can give it to you. But anyone can master the writing craft. It is a discipline like any other, requiring study, application and, above all, practice.

Clear writing comes from clear thinking and, conversely, muddled thinking results in muddled writing. So the first rule might well be said to be 'Think before you write'. It sounds almost so simple as to be insulting, yet how many executives complain that they have no time to think before they pour out endless memoranda on some subject or another. Organize the material in your mind before dictating it. Try to reduce it to a number of points and then put them down as succinctly and lucidly as possible. Finally, give your correspondent a clear indication of what you expect of him next. 'So what?' he may ask himself after carefully reading your analysis of a problem. If you need his instructions on what to do next, then clearly say so: 'I therefore look forward to receiving your further instructions.' Or: 'I would therefore appreciate receiving your advice on this problem.'

If, on the other hand, you have already resolved the problem in some way, then let him know: 'I have, therefore, decided to do such and such.' If you want to influence his decision, you must not fail to say so quite definitely: 'I therefore recommend that we proceed as follows:' Or you can make it even stronger: 'I therefore believe it is most important that we do such and such.'

Make your writing forceful and direct by preferring short Saxon words to the long Latin-derived ones. Use 'Begin' or 'Start' in preference to 'Commence'. Use 'Get up', 'Get down', 'Get Better', 'Get about', in place of their corresponding Latin-derived verbs. This combination of verb and adverb is a characteristic of the English language and much more forceful. There are hundreds of such combinations and your English can do nothing but improve if you make a point of seeking them out and using them.

Beware of long words with prefixes or suffixes, such as *pre, re, de,* or *ousness* and *ization*. They can often be replaced by two short words or even one short word of Saxon origin. Instead of being in a *predicament*, for instance, you could be in *trouble* and instead of having a *predilection* for long words you could cultivate a *liking* for short ones.

Together with short words, you would do well to favour short sentences, since it has been proven that short words and short sentences lead to better understanding of the written word.

The English sentence has been getting shorter and shorter over the centuries, so in adopting a short sentence, you will not only make your letters easier to understand, but you will give your English a more up-to-date garb. Short sentences encourage clear thinking. Make yours as short as possible at first. Gradually, over the months and the years, you will find them lengthening slightly without loss of clarity – you will be moving on to Stage 2 in your efforts to write better English. Your ultimate aim will be to vary the length of your sentences for greater variety and flexibility.

In selecting your words, then, you will go for the short rather than the long, the simple rather than the complex. In addition, you will choose the strong, colourful words and active verbs. You will only use the passive voice if you have to. Far too many top executives have the habit of writing: 'It has been decided.' How much more forceful to say: 'We have decided,' or 'The Board has decided.' The use of the passive voice in a sentence of this sort has a faint suggestion of the writer wanting to hold something back. 'It' never does anything. It is always a person or a group who do, feel, decide, think, and so on. Make this person or group the subject of your sentence whenever possible.

Cultivate the habit of looking up the word you want to use in the dictionary. You will be surprised to find how often the word does not mean *exactly* what you want to say. For instance, *verbal* means 'in words', as in: 'He did not give a verbal assent, but merely nodded.' It is often wrongly used for *oral*, i.e. spoken as distinct from written.

Some words are worked to death. We take a fancy to a word and then misuse it at will. A case in point is the word *bottleneck*. We read of bottlenecks being *reduced, solved, overcome,* or even *ironed out.* Bearing in mind that a bottleneck is a narrow space, it follows that the things you can do to it are severely limited. You can *cause* a bottleneck or *eliminate* one. Likewise, having caused a bottleneck, it is wisest to leave it at that, rather than attempting to make it sound more dramatic by writing about *severe* or *acute* bottlenecks.

In choosing an adjective, try to find one that conveys the exact shade of meaning you want. *Nice* means absolutely nothing, of course, since we talk of a 'nice steak', a 'nice girl', a 'nice garden', and even a 'nice order'.

Once you begin to think in this way about words you will quickly realize that every word has to earn its keep. No word has a right to be in your letter unless it makes a contribution to your meaning. If you go over a letter word by word and ask yourself in each case what purpose that word serves, you will be surprised to see how many of them are quite superfluous. Cut them out ruthlessly. If a word does not contribute to making your meaning clearer it has no business to be there.

Business correspondence is simply choked with these unsightly weeds. Not merely single words, but whole sentences need to be thrown out in favour of more direct, forceful language.

Here are a few of these dreadful 'commercial English' clichés:

and oblige (as a close)	carefully noted
as and from	communication (instead of letter)
as per	complying with your request
as stated above	contents duly noted
assuring you of our best attention	deem it advisable
	desire to state
at an early date	due to the fact that
at hand	enclosed herewith
at the present time	enclosed please find
at this writing	esteemed favour
at your earliest convenience	even date
attached please find	favour (instead of letter)
avail yourself of this opportunity	has come to hand
	has gone forward
await the pleasure of a reply	has greatly helped
awaiting the favour of your further esteemed commands	have before me
	having regard to the fact
	herewith enclose
beg to acknowledge	herewith please find
beg to advise	hoping to be favoured
beg to announce	if and when
beg to remain (before complimentary close)	in answer to same
	in connection therewith

in due course
in receipt of
in reply to yours
in reply I wish to state
in the near future
in this connection
instant
kind favour
kindly advise
kindly be advised
kindly inform
meet with your approval
note from your letter
note with interest
note with pleasure
of even date
our records show
owing to the fact that
past favours
permit me to state
please advise
please be advised
please do not hesitate
please find enclosed
please note
please rest assured
proximo
pursuant to
recent date
referring to your favour
referring to yours
regarding your communica-
tion
regret to advise
regret to state
replying to your favour
replying to yours

said (e.g. said package)
same (used as a pronoun)
submit herewith
take pleasure in advising
take this opportunity
thank you kindly
thank you in advance
the writer
this is to advise you
to hand
trusting this will
ultimo
under separate cover
upon receipt of
valued favour
valued patronage
we are pleased to advise
we note
we take pleasure
well and truly
when and as
wherein we state
wish to acknowledge
wish to advise
wish to state
would advise
would state
would suggest
your esteemed communication
your esteemed favour
your favour to hand
your letter of even date
your valued inquiry
yours just to hand
yours of the fourth
yours to hand

If you rid your English of these barren words; if you write short sentences and use plain, forceful words; if you think before you write, you will not need to be over anxious about the rules of grammar. It is far more important to write as you speak, so that you come alive to your correspondent as he reads your letter.

Do not be afraid of using contractions, such as 'I'd be happy to send you so and so'. Use a conversational tone. There is absolutely no reason why a business letter should be pompous. However, in letter-writing as in office behaviour in general, you will do well to follow the house style. Some companies are more formal than others and some professions call for more formal letter-writing.

Above all, cultivate the 'you' approach. Try writing: 'You will be happy to learn that your order has been shipped today', rather than: 'We are please to inform you. . . .' and so on. Far too many business letters are peppered throughout with 'I's' and 'We's', as if the writer had no other thought but himself.

Capitalization: The modern trend is to cut down on capitalization. Capitalize:

1 Proper names of persons, countries, towns, cities, counties, rivers, mountains, lakes, seas, and oceans.

2 The names of months and days of the week.

3 The titles of books, plays, articles, magazines, chapters, speeches, operas, songs, etc., e.g. 'His last book was *Better Business Letters,*' 'Her favourite opera is *La Traviata.*'

4 The names of ships, houses, hotels, restaurants, inns, etc.

5 A common noun when it is used in conjunction with a proper name, e.g. Waterloo Bridge, Lake Louise, Mount Olympus. Or when it is used in place of a proper name, e.g. 'The Bank has 50 branches' – meaning Bank X.

6 A designation of rank or position when it is used in conjunction with a proper name, e.g. 'Captain Brown was always the first to arrive.' Or when it refers to a specific person, e.g. 'The Pope has just returned from New York.'

Do *not* capitalize:

1 A common noun when it is used to indicate a general class of person or thing, e.g. 'There are a great many universities in the United States of America.'

2 A designation of rank or position when it is used as a com-

mon noun, e.g. 'Most sales managers have spent several years on the road.'

3 The names of the various disciplines when used in a general sense, e.g. 'His favourite subjects are philosophy, psychology, and history.'

Punctuation: The vogue for shorter sentences results in less frequent use of punctuation marks, except, of course, the full stop, which will be used more often. It is wrong, however, to go on and on without a comma in sight, regardless of whether your sentence needs one for clarity. As a rule of thumb, you might say that if the omission of a comma alters the meaning, then put one in. You need a comma to separate a list of items, e.g. 'Our third floor boutique has an excellent stock of ladies' suits, dresses, coats, and rainwear.' A comma belongs before the 'and' in the example given, but is omitted when only two items are listed, e.g. 'Bread and butter'.

Many good writers do not enclose subordinate remarks between commas and if your meaning is perfectly clear, you can safely leave the commas out. However, you must do either one thing or the other, and not put a comma before the phrase while leaving it out at the end. Many people do this and it is an untidy habit. Write either: 'Our Midland representative, Mr David Ross, will be calling on you soon.' Or: 'Our Midland representative Mr David Ross will be calling on you soon.' This sentence clearly benefits from the insertion of a comma before and after 'Mr David Ross'. The following sentence needs the two commas even more: 'Mr Jackson, whom you met at our last sales conference, will be in town again next week.'

You should also use a comma before a direct quotation, e.g. 'He said, "I shall be back at 10".' A comma should also separate the remarks which come between a direct quotation, e.g. 'Don't be late', he said, 'or there'll be trouble'.

The semicolon is supposed to indicate a pause somewhat longer than a comma, but the modern short sentence has more or less retired it. In letter-writing especially, you seldom need to use a semicolon. If you find your sentence is so long that you have to break it up with semicolons, then you would do well to think again and re-write it in two or more shorter sentences.

However, if you are listing a number of items which fall naturally into several distinct groups, your sentence will be clearer if you divide each group with a semicolon and the items within the groups with a comma, e.g. 'Our Publishing House has three divisions: Technical Books, which covers works on engineering, electronics, physics, and automation; Business Books, which includes works on management, accounting, and office procedures; and Fiction, which includes novels, plays, and poetry'.

Sometimes the semicolon does indeed indicate a longer pause. This happens when you leave out a word. For instance, if you say: 'We have ten branches in the United Kingdom, but only two throughout the rest of the world', a comma will do admirably. But if you omit the word 'but', a longer pause will be needed and you will therefore need to use a semicolon in place of the comma, e.g. 'We have ten branches in the United Kingdom; only two throughout the rest of the world'.

The colon indicates a pause somewhat longer than a semicolon, but not quite so long as a full stop. You will seldom need to use it in business letters, or indeed, in personal letters. It can be used before a direct quotation, in place of a comma, and should be used before enumerations, examples, and explanations, e.g. 'The qualities we seek in our employees are: honesty, reliability, and industry.'

The full stop is the longest pause of all and should be used at the end of a sentence, after initials, and most abbreviations. If an abbreviation ends as a word normally does, then no full stop is necessary, e.g. Mr, Dr, Mme (no point).

The other punctuation marks are: the interrogation mark, the exclamation, inverted commas, the hyphen, parentheses, and the dash.

The interrogation mark is used only after a direct question, not after an indirect one. It can also be used between parentheses to indicate that a word or statement is in doubt.

Use the exclamation mark very sparingly. It means that the word or sentence which precedes it is charged with emotion. Some people use it out of sheer exuberance.

Inverted commas are used before and after direct speech.

The hyphen is used to unite two separate words into a compound one. In time, such compound words become one and the hyphen is dropped.

I

Some people scatter dashes all through their letters in place of other punctuation marks. They feel a pause is needed but cannot remember whether it should be a comma, a semicolon, or a full stop – so in goes a dash. Rightfully, a dash should only be used to signify a sudden break in the reasoning, the resumption of a scattered subject, or an omission, such as a naughty word. Here are some examples:

'I could go on and on – but there goes the dinner bell and I must close.'
'Dogs, cats, mice, rats – all were there.'
'I told him that if he didn't like it, he could —— lump it.'
Use your dashes sparingly, as a good cook uses her spices.

Take a letter, please: You are now ready to start dictating that friendly yet lucid and concise letter which can do so much to oil the wheels of both business and social life. Like most business-men, you will probably have a capable secretary to do the physical work for you and in half-an-hour you can dictate as many letters as it would take you the whole morning to write yourself. Social customs have eased to the point where it is now considered perfectly correct to type personal letters. This means that you can dictate those, too. Only replies to invitations sent to your home, condolence letters, and 'bread and butter' letters need be written by hand.

So few people nowadays can spare the time to write personal letters by hand and, furthermore, so many people have such an illegible scrawl that the typewritten letter has become not merely acceptable, but, in some cases, eminently desirable.

If you want to give your business letters a more personal touch, you can 'top and tail' them, that is, write in by hand the 'Dear Mr So-and-So' and the complimentary close.

The rule for beginning and ending letters is very simple. If you begin a letter 'Dear Sir' or 'Dear Sirs', then you close 'Yours faithfully'. If you begin 'Dear Mr Smith', then you end 'Yours sincerely' or 'Sincerely yours'.

When it comes to personal letters beginning 'Dear Bob' or 'Dear Jane', there is absolutely no reason why you should not end them exactly as you wish. You should feel no compulsion to write a formal close. George Bernard Shaw, who wrote hun-dreds, perhaps thousands, of beautiful letters, almost always said his piece and then signed off. Or perhaps he wrote: 'Good night, fair sorceress' to Ellen Terry. She, in turn, chose the most beguiling endings as befitted a 'sorceress' of her ilk. Both Shaw and Ellen Terry were being true to themselves and that is what you must be in your personal letters. Forget about formal endings and just be yourself. Your correspondents will like you the better for it.

Chapter 8 gives you all the information you need to address titled and eminent people, as well as anyone else who is not just a plain 'Mister'. However, as mentioned in that chapter, the very formal, flowery endings are no longer used, except in the case of the Queen. 'Yours faithfully' nowadays is good enough for anyone, or almost anyone. Needless to say, you should sign all your letters. A rubber stamp is simply not good enough.

If you are writing a personal letter to someone's business address, it is perfectly in order to mark the envelope 'Personal'. If you write to his home, however, it is not polite to mark it 'Personal', since the assumption is that, being addressed to him, he will himself open it.

If you hand a letter over to someone to deliver personally, it is customary to leave it unsealed. The person then usually seals it himself in your presence. You may, however, make an exception to this rule if, for instance, the envelope contains something that is likely to slip out. In such a case, it is polite to explain to your messenger why you had to seal the envelope. None of this, of course, applies to business letters entrusted to a paid messenger.

The courtesy letter

However busy you may be dictating your business correspondence, you will at times want to spare the few moments required to write a really sincere letter of apology, a note of introduction for a friend, a letter congratulating a friend on an achievement, a thank-you letter, or a letter of condolence.

Some of these letters *must* be written, however difficult you may find them, while others are a matter of thoughtfulness and generosity.

The note of apology: We have already seen in the previous

chapter how to turn down a formal invitation. It sometimes happens, however, that you have accepted an invitation, fully intend to go, and then something quite unexpectedly prevents you from doing so. The polite thing to do is to telephone or telegraph immediately, so that your hostess is inconvenienced as little as possible, and to write a short letter as well. You might say something like this:

Dear Mrs Brown,
    I apologize most sincerely for having to wire you as I did about Saturday evening.
    I was recalled both urgently and unexpectedly to Head Office and there was nothing for it but to go. My telegram did seem ungrateful after you had so kindly offered me the hospitality of your home during my all too brief visit to Reading.
    I was sorry indeed not to be with you.
              Yours sincerely,
                John Harris

Of course, should the invitation have been for you and your wife, then she would have written.

The letter of introduction: You no doubt frequently have occasion to write a letter introducing a business acquaintance to another one and such letters are probably second nature to you. Occasionally, however, you will want to give a note of introduction to a personal friend for purely social purposes. You would do well in such cases to be quite sure that the two people involved will enjoy each other's company, otherwise you risk losing both friendships. Once you decide to write such a letter, however, it presents no complication at all. You might say:

Dear Jim,
    I have taken the liberty of giving your name and address to my old friend and schoolmate, Edwin Forster, who will be visiting Scotland early next month for a short holiday.
    Edwin is a very keen golfer, as well as a fine *raconteur* with a seemingly inexhaustible supply of good

yarns. I therefore anticipate that you will get on well together and thoroughly enjoy each other's company.

I shall certainly appreciate any kindness you
extend to Edwin.

Sincerely,

Letters of congratulations: There is nothing any of us likes receiving more than a letter of congratulations for an achievement,
a milestone in our career or private life, a promotion, or any
other suitable occasion. Yet so few of us bother to offer this
satisfaction to a friend or business associate. It takes only a few
minutes and is perfectly simple to do. To a business friend newly
appointed to the board of directors of his company, you might
write:

Dear Mr Watson,

I have just read in *The Times* of your
appointment to the Wagstaff Board and hasten to send you
my most sincere congratulations.

I am quite convinced that the Board will
be strengthened by your inclusion and your Company is to
be congratulated for its acumen in selecting the right man
for the job.

Yours sincerely,
Bill Brown

Thank-you letters: There are many occasions when it is courteous
to write a note of thanks, even though you have already expressed
your appreciation in person. If a business friend has kindly set
aside some of his valuable time to address your staff at the
annual sales conference, for instance, he deserves more than just
a verbal 'Thank You'.

You could write something like this:

Dear George,

Now that the dust has settled and we are back
at home base, I want to tell you once again how very much
my colleagues and I appreciated your generous contribution
to our Sales Conference.

I heard nothing but enthusiastic comments on
your talk and the men were quite obviously impressed. If

sales go up by leaps and bounds, I'll know who to blame!
                Once again, many thanks and best wishes for
1967.

                                        Sincerely,
                                  Mark Pierson

If you have spent a week-end or longer at the home of friends, then good manners demand that you write a 'bread-and-butter' letter in addition to your verbally-expressed thanks. Such letters are usually written by one wife to the other wife, but there are many exceptions when business friends are involved and, obviously, when there is no wife in the picture.

Suppose, for instance, you had been invited to spend a week-end at a customer's villa during your business trip to Italy. If your trip was a very brief one, you would write after your return to home base. If it was a very extended trip, however, you would have to drop a brief note immediately upon resuming your journey.

In the first eventuality, you might write your hostess something like this:

Dear Signora Bianchi,
                Back in London after a most successful trip, I should like to thank you most sincerely for the wonderful hospitality shown me at the Villa Fiorita.
                Certainly my stay at your country home stands out as a highlight of my trip.
                It was really most kind of you to offer me such generous hospitality.
                        Yours sincerely,
                        George Stewart

Letters of Condolence: These are, perhaps, the most difficult letters to write. It is best to make them quite brief, since once you have conveyed the idea that you feel for the bereaved person, additional words can do nothing to alleviate the pain.

If your best customer lost his chairman, you might write to the managing director (assuming, of course, that your relationship with him warranted it):

Dear Mr Green,

        I was distressed to read in this morning's issue of *The Times* of the sudden tragic death of your Chairman.

        I know that his loss will be keenly felt by your Company and I want to assure you of my deepest sympathy.

Yours sincerely,
William Brown

Over 900 specimen letters for all occasions are given in my last book, written especially for the businessman who wants to improve his letter writing.*

* *Personal Letters for Businessmen*. Mary Bosticco, Business Publications Limited, Second Edition, 1966.

chapter eleven

making a speech

The managing director of a fair-sized manufacturing company rose to introduce the new chairman to the assembled staff, gathered together from every branch. 'I won't bore you with his background,' he announced genially, 'because I don't know it.'

One wonders what the staff thought of their M.D. at that moment, but there is very little doubt as to what the new chairman thought! Unquestionably the M.D. would have found it to his advantage to master the art of speaking in public with courtesy, tact, and skill.

There is surely not a single businessman who is not called upon with at least moderate frequency to express himself in public. Yet how few of them acquit themselves worthily. Some of them are quite aware of their inadequacy, yet do not bother to do anything about it.

How well do *you* do on the speaker's platform? If you do not shine, it would certainly pay you to improve your performance. Many useful books have been written on the subject, although best results are obtained through taking one of the many courses which are available.

The secret of success is organization and preparation. It is surprising how many executives will hurriedly dictate a few notes at the very last minute and rush to a meeting without as much as a single rehearsal. No wonder they do such a poor job.

But there is an ingredient which is even more important for success as a public speaker. Without it no one can hope to succeed, yet unlike organization and preparation, it is not there for the asking. This all-important ingredient is sincerity. Everyone recognizes its presence, for it shines through every word that is said. Conversely, everyone notices its absence.

Some executives do not 'come across' in their speeches. They make no impression, leave their audience cold. Why? Because they lack that all important ingredient – sincerity.

Yet you cannot enjoin anyone to 'be sincere', in spite of some very famous books on salesmanship. You are either sincere or else you are not. If you are not, you can be quite certain that you will not fool everyone.

A sincere person is free of pretence, hyprocrisy, sham, show, arrogance, and equivocation. A sincere person truly believes what he says and his sincerity is irresistible.

If you have something worthwhile to say, if you truly believe in it, if you organize your talk well and make adequate preparation, i.e. rehearse it well, you cannot fail as a public speaker.

Types of speech

How you decide to deliver your speech will depend partly on the circumstances and partly on your personal preference. There are four broad types of speech:

1 THE IMPROMPTU OR EXTEMPORE SPEECH This is the hardest of all, since it has to be thought up on the spur of the moment. It is the kind of talk you give when unexpectedly asked to 'say a few words'. A great many executives frequently have to speak to small or large groups unexpectedly and, after several years of experience, become quite adept at it.

2 THE PREPARED SPEECH, DELIVERED FROM NOTES This is the best possible way to tackle a speech, because the words you use are spontaneous and there is not that terrible risk inherent

in memorizing the whole speech. The secret of success lies in using the right kind of notes. Cue-cards are the very best solution. Put your whole talk down on paper, double-spaced. Read it over, preferably aloud, two or three times, then write down on small cards the main points in chronological order. Number your cards consecutively, then try making your speech by referring to your cards only. If you forget something, add it to the card, in the appropriate place. Continue to rehearse your talk aloud from the cards until you do it correctly, without leaving anything out.

When the day dawns and you get up to make your speech, do not conceal your cards, they are nothing to be ashamed of. Simply turn them over as you finish with them. You will find they give you tremendous self-confidence. You *know* you cannot be stumped, and the words will come easily, since you will have rehearsed your talk many times, using alternative words.

This method is ideal for most business situations.

3 THE READ SPEECH This results in a rather dreary performance, unless undertaken by a first-class actor. The language is inclined to be written rather than spoken English, the speaker loses eye contact with his audience and even skilled speakers are apt to send their audiences to sleep when they resort to reading their speeches. None the less, the written speech is indispensable in certain situations when absolute accuracy is imperative, such as giving a report at a shareholders' meeting. Even in such cases, however, if you possibly can, you should deliver some parts of the speech from notes and only read those portions concerned with facts and figures.

4 THE MEMORIZED SPEECH This is an excellent method, particularly for very short addresses and if you are skilful enough not to make it sound 'memorized'. It does have a tremendous drawback, however, and that is, that if you forget a 'line', you're sunk. In point of fact, if you are using method 2 you usually end up by memorizing a good deal of the speech, but without running the risk of drying up.

The parts of a speech

A talk, like a letter, should have a beginning, a middle, and an
end. It should flow logically from A to B to C, carrying the
audience along with it. This logical progression goes as follows:

1 THE CLARION CALL This serves to wake the audience up and
   gain their attention. You might call it the heigh-ho, since in
   effect it says: 'Heigh-ho there, listen to me.' It is a vital part
   of your speech, since if you do not have your audience's
   attention, you might just as well leave your talk unsaid.

2 THE PROPOSITION Here you state your case.

3 THE EVIDENCE Here you bring in the facts and figures which
   prove your case.

4 THE CONCLUSIONS Here you show what conclusions can be
   drawn from the facts you have presented.

5 THE 'SO-WHAT' Here you tell your audience what you want
   them to do about it, or exhort them to take action, according
   to the circumstances.

The learned experts have far higher-sounding names for the
various parts of the speech, of course. The 'So-What', for instance,
is none other than the peroration of the legal profession. But
there is absolutely nothing to be gained from pomposity and the
more informal and friendly we make our talks, the more effective
they will be. Bringing the terms down to earth is an excellent
beginning.

Quite frequently you will find yourself making a speech which
is not really trying to sell anything. You may simply be reporting
on the activities of your department during the year gone by.
In such cases you will still need your 'Clarion Call' to start off
with, your 'Proposition' may simply be that your department has
increased its sales by 15 per cent, your 'Evidence' will be a mention of some of the most interesting orders, and your 'conclusion'
the hope to do even better in the following year. In all probability
there will be no 'So-What'.

There are very many other cases in which a speech does not

follow the pattern outlined, but so long as you start off with your
'Clarion Call', continue logically with your report, company
history or whatever it is, and then make sure to end with a crystal-
clear 'So-What', if there is one, you will make a competent, easy-
to-follow speech.

How to begin

In Britain, it is still customary to begin a speech with the words
'Ladies and Gentlemen', or 'Mr Chairman, Gentlemen', not to
mention the far more convoluted forms. Some people even maintain that this is an admirable custom, since the speaker does not
have to worry about what his first words are to be and can pull
himself together while he utters them!

Unfortunately, however, these forms are both dull and stiff
with formality. Nothing, in fact, could be more conducive to
stretching one's legs forward and taking a little nap.

Public-speaking pupils in the U.S.A. are taught simply to begin,
without a preamble of any sort. This permits a lively, cheerful
note to be struck right away. It permits the speaker to get close
to his audience from the word 'go', without the cold formal
barrier of 'Ladies and Gentlemen'. Ladies and Gentlemen are
passé, anyway, so if you have the courage, just get up and begin.
No one will hold it against you. There *are*, of course, occasions
when the formality is a 'must', but such occasions will undoubtedly make themselves felt.

Parts 2, 3, 4, and 5 of your speech will depend entirely on your
material. Part 1, the 'Clarion Call' or 'Heigh-ho' gives you plenty
of scope to use your imagination. There are a number of different
openings you can use, according to your personality, the occasion
and the type of talk you are giving. Here are some of them:

> 1 THE COMPLIMENT You say how happy you are to be there, to
> see them all, to see them all again, to see *so many more of*
> *them*, to see them all again *at last*, or whatever the case may
> be. This is an excellent opening, since it pleases your audience
> and you're starting off on the right foot by referring to *them*,
> the most important subject in their eyes. If you decide to

scrap the 'Ladies and Gentlemen' prop, raise your arms to your audience and say 'Hello, Everybody' instead, you can then launch straight into the complimentary form of opening with great success. By then, you can be quite sure they'll all be awake and listening. However, such a breezy, informal opening is obviously only suitable for certain occasions, such as a sales conference, when it can be highly successful.

2 THE JOKE This is a very common form of opening and there is no better way of beginning a speech than by getting a laugh. It should be handled with care by the beginner, however, as it is not so easy as it sounds. If the joke is relevant to your theme, so much the better.

3 THE STORY This is very similar to the joke opening, except that it is not a joke! Everyone loves a story and providing it is relevant to your theme, it is a good opening gambit.

4 THE STARTLING FACT This can be an excellent attention-getter, but it is slightly more suited to the fund-rasing speech or one which aims at making converts. If you were preaching population control, for instance, you could start off by saying: 'If the population of the world continues to grow at its present alarming rate, it will be standing room only by the year 2000.' That should wake them up. You can then amplify the point a little to drive it home before launching on the body of your talk and you're off to a good start.

5 THE QUOTATION Here you start off by quoting one of the classics, a witty quip, a well-known personality or a previous speaker, as appropriate. At business conferences this can often be arranged beforehand with the speaker appearing before you. If, for instance, the speaker before you has outlined the company's marketing strategy for the coming year and you are scheduled to explain how you plan to carry out your part of it, you can start off by saying: 'As Joe Doakes has just told us, we are aiming at increasing turnover by 25 per cent this year. The advertising budget has been increased accordingly and I'd like to tell you a little more about this side of our plans for the year ahead.'

6 CHRISTMAS AGAIN With the kind of talk that takes place regularly every year, such as Christmas staff parties or shareholders' meetings, you can begin by referring to the occasion itself, thanking your audience for their support during the past year or expressing any other appropriate sentiment.

7 THE APPEAL TO SELF-INTEREST This one is particularly useful if your talk aims to 'sell' something, whether an idea or an actual commodity or service. You can even cheat a little here without doing any lasting harm, particularly if the audience has been passed to you half-asleep by a previous

'. . . or otherwise creating a stir'

speaker. 'How many of you would like to double your income overnight?' That should wake them up. When you see them sitting up and taking notice, you can go on to say, 'Well, I'm afraid I can't quite tell you how to do *that*, but I can tell you how to increase your sales considerably' or whatever the case may be. This kind of opening is always effective. If you can think how your proposition can help your audience and you present that benefit in a few words at the very opening of your speech, you will be giving them an excellent reason for listening to you.

8 THE VISUAL AID Why not start right off with a visual aid? One very successful professional speaker used to start off his talk on motivation by presenting his audience with a chart reading:

```
MONEY

BUILDINGS

MACHINERY

MEN
```

'Which of these would you say was the most important?' he would ask. Then after a pause: 'You all know the answer—men, of course.' And he would go on to explain how men are a business's most important asset.

9 THE GIMMICK Here you walk on to the platform doing something or carrying something or otherwise creating a stir. You then casually ask: 'I suppose you're wondering why I'm standing on my head?' Or 'I suppose you're wondering what this curious object is?' Or 'Why I'm wearing this huge pair of rose-tinted spectacles' or whatever. Then you go on to explain why or what it's all about. This type of opening is an excellent attention-getter and if you have a bit of the ham in you, why not try it some time? One very effective

speaker used to march up to the platform brandishing a three-legged stool which he proceeded to wave at his audience. 'I suppose you're wondering what this has got to do with my talk?' he'd ask his audience with a Puckish smile. 'Well, it happens to be a milking-stool and farmers where I come from have been using them for centuries. The three legs give it a very solid foundation and I'm now going to show you how the three principles on which my technique is based give it an equally solid foundation.'

Our Puckish orator almost had a visual aid in his milking-stool, but perhaps his 'Heigh-Ho' was a hybrid between the gimmick and the visual aid.

There are other ways of beginning and, no doubt, you can think of several yourself. You can also combine two or even three of the suggested openings, as we have seen. If you make a great number of speeches it would be well worth your while to keep a scrapbook of apt quotations, jokes, anecdotes, and arresting statistics on your usual subjects. You will then have a mine of new ideas on how to begin your talks.

Delivery

It goes without saying that you will present yourself impeccably groomed on the speaker's platform. Not only will this give you added confidence, but it will inspire confidence in your audience.

Try speaking to the people in the last row of the auditorium. Address yourself to them and you stand a better chance of being heard. Should a microphone be provided, make sure you have an opportunity of trying it out and becoming familiar with it beforehand.

Enunciate your words clearly, without slurring or hurrying. Try to look cheerful and smile as you approach the platform. Above all, look at your audience. Eye-contact with your audience is just about the most important aspect of delivery.

A good plan is to approach the platform with a smile, or rise with a smile if you are sitting on a rostrum. Look your audience straight in the eye for a few seconds, continue to smile at them, and then begin. You might start by looking at the back row, then shift your gaze further forward, to the right and to the left, and continue to maintain your eye contact all the way through your talk.

Mannerisms to avoid

Your arms should be in repose when you start off, but as you warm to your subject you will find them gesturing naturally. Fashions in gestures seem to change and one year's popular gesture seems to become next year's taboo. Everyone seems to agree, at least, that fidgeting is best avoided. This includes buttoning and unbuttoning your jacket, brushing back your locks, fiddling with paper clips or shuffling your notes unnecessarily, sticking your hands in your pockets and jingling your coins or keys. Acrobatics are also frowned on in the best circles, yet there was at least one much-beloved lecturer who got himself and his chair into all manner of extraordinary positions without any harm either to himself or his audience.

Standing with legs apart, while you clutch the lapels of your jacket is not to be recommended, neither is clasping your hands in front of you. The latter pose is dubbed 'the fig leaf' in the u.s.a. In Britain, clasping the hands behind seems to be very well regarded, no doubt because it is the favourite pose of members of the Royal Family of both sexes.

In point of fact, however, the very best thing you can do with your arms is perhaps the most difficult thing, i.e. to let them just hang, as it were. It requires poise and self-control, but it looks beautifully relaxed. As mentioned, as your talk progresses you will find your arms moving of their own accord – that is, if you really feel what you're saying and have at least some semblance of temperament, they will do so. There should be no need for you deliberately to move your arms here or there.

Ingredients of the successful speech

Quite apart from content, there are several things you can do to help ensure the success of your talk. The most important of all is:

The 'You' approach: This involves writing your speech from your audience's point of view. What will your proposition do for

K

them? What is there in it for them? Think of your material from their point of view and cast your talk accordingly. Cut down on your 'I''s and 'We''s and say 'You' instead. Don't say: 'I'm happy to tell you', but 'You'll be happy to learn.'

In addition, hold your audience by:

Being positive: You will not inspire your audience by telling them how unworthy you are to speak on the subject, how little time you had to prepare, or that you left your notes behind. If all of these things are true, then you have no business being there at all and the audience knows it. So always remember to accent the positive and leave your blushing modesty behind.

Showing enthusiasm: Enthusiasm is catching. If you really believe in your subject, let the audience see it. Nothing is more stimulating and more endearing than enthusiasm.

Make use of visual aids: The importance of visual aids in holding an audience's attention cannot be overstressed. Luckily, there is scarcely a subject which you cannot bring home more clearly with graphs, charts, illustrations, or other visual aids. So important is the visual aid in holding an audience's attention that you will find it well worth while to bring in an illustration, even if you have to bend over backwards to do so.

Strive for audience participation: Nothing is more likely to keep your audience attentive than giving them something to do. Do try it, even if it is something quite trivial, such as asking: 'How many of you would agree with that?' or 'How many of you are here for the first time?' or any other relevant question. If you can get your audience participating you can almost be sure that your talk will be a success.

What to say

Luckily, as a businessman, you will seldom have to worry about what to say in your talks. Your task will stand quite clearly before you and all you will need worry about is how to organize your talk, how to deliver it, and how best to secure your audience's attention.

Sometimes, however, other speaking occasions will come your

way and you, too, will become involved in what might be termed the ritual speech. Such talks include presentations to retiring employees, official openings of hospitals, bazaars, or flower shows, prize-givings at schools or at social events, introducing a speaker, accepting an office, and after-dinner speeches.

Such talks call for sincerity, simplicity, courtesy, and generosity. Brevity is also appreciated. A good plan to follow for such talks is to go from the general to the particular. In opening a new branch, for instance, you could begin by stressing the company's past achievements and then go on to say how this particular new branch will contribute to future growth. In opening a bazaar, you might begin by saying something pleasant about the particular charity involved and then go on to dwell on the co-operation and teamwork which has made the bazaar possible. Here are some further suggestions:

Presentation to departing employee: This is an occasion which calls for a gracious compliment, not an assessment of the person's merits and demerits. Single out the person's main qualities connected with his job and praise him graciously and generously on them. Say what the gift is and why it is being presented and finally make the presentation.

Accepting a presentation: Modesty and sincerity are the keynotes here. Do not be afraid of showing your feelings, but do not be dragged into saying anything you do not mean. Express your thanks and gratitude as simply as you can. Explain what has been your guiding philosophy in the years of service you have given. Express appreciation for the gift and end by repeating your thanks.

Accepting an office: You might begin by saying 'Thank you' for the honour conferred on you. You could then go on to say something about the work of the organization in general, its principles as you see them and how you intend to uphold them when you take up the office.

Introducing a speaker: Begin with a word of welcome to the speaker. Go on to say why he or she is especially well qualified to speak on the subject and end with: 'Ladies and Gentlemen, Mr Brian Cooper.' Above all, make it brief. Don't steal your speaker's thunder by anticipating what he is going to say. He will not thank you for it.

Proposing a vote of thanks: You can make this very brief indeed and simply say that you are delighted to propose a vote of thanks to Mr Cooper for his most enlightening talk. There are occasions, however, when it would be courteous to say a little more. If the occasion is a school concert or amateur performance of some sort, it is thoughtful to say how excellent the performance was, how very much you and the rest of the audience enjoyed it and to thank everyone for the hard work they put into it. You can end either by wishing the Dramatic Society – or whatever the case may be – every success in the future, or by saying how very much you and the rest of the audience appreciated their efforts.

After-dinner speeches: At official dinners, the first speeches are always the loyal toasts. They are proposed by the chairman and have to follow a prescribed form, approved by the Queen. At the moment, only two loyal toasts are authorized: the Queen, and other members of the Royal Family.

The proposer of the loyal toasts is not required to make a speech. He simply rises and says: 'Ladies and Gentlemen – the Queen!' whereupon the guests also rise, repeat: 'The Queen', raise their glasses and drink.

The toast to other members of the Royal Family is not proposed quite so frequently, but has also to follow the approved formula, which is altered periodically by Buckingham Palace in accordance with changes within the Royal Family.

Most other toasts at formal dinners or luncheons are preceded by a speech and are proposed by speakers appointed in advance. Proposer and responder are called upon to play their part by the chairman or the toastmaster, if there is one.

At formal dinners, the responder is not supposed to propose another toast, but on less formal occasions this is frequently done. At wedding receptions, for instance, the bridegroom replies to the toast to the bride and bridegroom and usually ends by proposing a toast to the bridesmaids.

If you decide to accept an invitation to make an after-dinner speech, you will probably find the task far harder than that of giving the usual kind of business talk. The after-dinner speech requires an effort of the imagination. It should amuse and entertain the listeners. Certainly you will not want to undertake the task lightly. The following guide-lines may help you:

1 Do your homework. Find out from the person who invited you to speak or from the secretary of the organization holding the event, how many people are expected, whether women will be present, what *kind* of people they will be, i.e. a very dignified gathering, a sporting crowd or a local affair. You will also need to know how long you will be expected to speak, at what point you will be speaking, i.e. before or in between musical entertainment, the size of the room, whether or not there will be a microphone and whether there is anything the organizers particularly want you to mention, or indeed, leave out.

This information will enable you to prepare and rehearse your speech carefully beforehand, leaving you free during the dinner to enjoy both it and the company and in turn to be a pleasant guest.

2 Make sure that your speech has a theme, that it makes a valid point which your listeners can remember and ponder upon afterwards.

3 Stick to your own last. If you are to propose a toast to 'Our Distinguished Guest', then stick to that and resist the temptation to wander on to other subjects, or even worse, to poach on another speaker's territory.

4 Relate your speech to the gathering. Not only should your speech have a theme, but it should tie in with the occasion. A little thought and imagination should enable you to think up something both amusing and apt. If you can fit yourself as speaker into the picture also, this will be all to the good.

5 Make your speech bright, cheerful, and humorous, if you can. If you plan to do a lot of after-dinner speaking, it will certainly pay you to keep a scrapbook of amusing anecdotes for such occasions, as mentioned previously.

6 Address your speech to the chairman. At the same time, make sure that everyone can hear you clearly above the din of coffee cups, *sotto voce* conversation, and bustling waiters. Take your time, speak clearly and distinctly and resist at all

costs the temptation to hum and haw. The moment you catch yourself doing it, stop short, think of your word, then say it.

7 As with any kind of speech, you must be positive. Do not apologize. Nothing could be duller than to announce that you have no idea why you were chosen for this particular toast, or how unworthy of the task you feel, how unaccustomed you are to public speaking, or indeed that you have a cold and had to rush unprepared into the breach.

As for what to say, this boils down, in nine cases out of ten, to something complimentary. If your toast is 'The Association', then obviously you will have found out all about it and you will speak of its purpose and activities. If your toast is 'Our Guest', then he is the man you will eulogize. If it is 'The Ladies', you will lean over backwards to say something pleasant about the fair sex. As a businessman, you might say something about what an important section of the market they are and what an influence they have on spending the family money. However, a little gallantry would no doubt be more welcome. This toast, incidentally, usually falls to the youngest bachelor present and does not call for a reply.

If you are scheduled to reply to a toast, your task will be even harder, for, obviously, you will not be able to prepare beforehand, to any great extent. All you will be able to do is listen very carefully to the proposer and then model your reply on his words.

As for the length of your talks, you should keep to the exact time allotted to you at official functions, since they are timed to the minute. On other occasions, you would do well to talk for five or ten minutes less than requested. No one ever complained that a talk was too short.

chapter twelve

meetings and committees

As a businessman, you will be unlikely to get by without ever attending a formal meeting conducted along lines similar to Parliamentary procedure. This may happen not only in your business life, but also in your political, cultural, or social activities. Whether or not you actually hold office, you will need to be familiar with the procedure.

The chairman

The chairman is clearly the most important man where meetings are concerned, and except when the chief executive of a company is presiding or where someone by virtue of his office takes the chair as a matter of course, the first business of a body meeting for the first time is to appoint a chairman.

This is usually done by someone rising and saying: 'I propose that Mr A be nominated as chairman.' Someone else then rises and says: 'I second that', whereupon everyone voices assent and Mr A becomes chairman on a unanimous vote.

It is quite unusual for the chairmanship of an ordinary business or social meeting to be contested, as the person proposed is

usually decided upon beforehand. But should there be a difference of opinion, the proceedings then become somewhat more
formal and a temporary chairman is proposed. This is custom-
arily done in the form of a motion, i.e. 'That Mr B do take the
chair.' The motion is then seconded, as we have seen before, and
put to the vote.

No difficulty is usually experienced in appointing a temporary
chairman, since his sole function is that of securing the election
of the permanent chairman and his role is ended as soon as one
has been elected. Moreover, he cannot himself be nominated for
the permanent chairmanship.

Having taken the chair, the temporary chairman will rise and
say: 'Ladies and gentlemen, I shall now be happy to receive
nominations for the post of chairman.' He will usually set a time
limit for each speaker, three minutes being the time frequently
allowed.

Someone will then rise and formally propose a candidate,
following his motion by a few words about his candidate's suit-
ability for the post. When the first speaker has finished, one of
his friends or a friend of the proposed candidate will second the
proposal and the way is now clear for others to put forward their
own candidates.

The temporary chairman collects all nominations and when
no more are forthcoming he puts each one to the vote, either in
the order in which they were made or in alphabetical order, as
previously agreed. The voting is usually by a show of hands. If
the first nomination is not carried, the number of 'Ayes' is
counted and noted. Voting then proceeds for the second and
subsequent candidates.

If no nomination is carried, it is usual to call to the chair the
candidate securing the largest number of votes. Another and
fairer method is to eliminate the candidate with the fewest 'Ayes'
and put the remaining candidates to the vote again. This procedure can be repeated until a clear majority is arrived at.

A person nominated as chairman must have given his prior
consent and must be present at the election meeting. There is
nothing to stop a nominee from voting for himself as chairman,
although it may be more advisable for him to remain strictly
neutral, especially if the chairmanship is being hotly contested.

Once elected, it is the chairman's duty to proceed with the

business of the meeting. A chairman's first requisite is that he be thoroughly familiar not only with the proper conduct of meetings, but also with the bye-laws of the organization concerned, or, if it is a company meeting, with the company's articles of association.

He should conduct meetings with strict impartiality, tact, courtesy, and firmness. He should remain alert and attentive throughout the meeting, listening to each speaker courteously and speaking as he would wish others to speak. He is not expected to be without an opinion, but rather to keep it to himself and resist the temptation of favouring those in the meeting whose views he shares. He should be quick and fair in his judgment and firm in keeping order and in holding the meeting to its purpose.

More specifically, the chairman's duties are:

1 To make sure that the meeting has been correctly convened.

2 To make sure that a quorum is present, according to the bye-laws of the organization, or the company's articles of association.

3 To state the purpose of the meeting.

4 To have the minutes of the previous meeting read. This is usually done by the secretary.

5 To have any correspondence read. This is also a task for the secretary.

6 To proceed with the business set down on the agenda.

7 To close the meeting.

The secretary

After the chairman, the secretary is just about the most important official in an organization, whether it be a company, a society, or other body – at least, as far as the conduct of a meeting is concerned. Of course, there are secretaries and secretaries and we are not concerned here with the duties of a company secretary as such, any more than we were concerned before with the duties of a company chairman as such. What we shall review are the duties of the secretary, whether honorary or paid, at meetings.

The secretary's first duty will be to send out notices of the meeting, if called for, or otherwise to display the notice in a prominent place. He will then need to work out the agenda and in some instances he will send a copy of it to each participant.

The agenda of a meeting usually follows a fairly regular form, as follows:

1 Minutes of the last meeting.

2 Matters arising from the minutes.

3 Correspondence (this often consists of letters of apology from members unable to attend).

4 Reports.

5 Election of officers for the ensuing year (if applicable).

6 Any other business.

Obviously, in preparing an agenda the secretary would mention which reports were to be presented and any other important matter to be discussed, lumping together only trivial matters under 'Any other business'.

When the day of the meeting dawns, the secretary will first of all make sure that arrangements for the reception and comfort of the members have been taken care of and then he will take his seat on the platform next to the chairman. From then on he will act as the chairman's right-hand man, keeping documents handy for him when he wants them and having facts at his finger-tips. He will also pay close attention to the proceedings and take notes of all decisions made and, in general, of the conduct of the meeting. His notes will serve him in good stead when he comes to writing up the minutes of the meeting.

At the beginning of the meeting, the chairman will call upon him to read the notice convening the meeting and then again to read the minutes of the previous meeting, as well as any correspondence.

The minutes of a meeting should be very carefully written if they are accurately to reflect what actually happened. Minutes of club and society meetings are often very casually written and include only the decisions made. The minutes of directors' meetings, however, must conform to the provisions of the Companies Act, 1948 and include the appointment of officers made by the directors, the names of the directors present, and all the resolutions and proceedings.

It is a good plan to adopt a pattern for the minutes, as this makes them much easier both to write and to read. The following is a reasonable plan:

1 Place, date, and time the meeting began.

2 The name of the chairman.

3 The name of other officials present, as well as all others present, in the case of a small organization, or the number of members present, in the case of larger bodies.

4 Reference to the formalities gone through before the actual business of the meeting, i.e. reading of notice of meeting and minutes of previous meeting and so on.

5 An outline of the business transacted and decisions made.

6 Date fixed for the next meeting, if applicable.

7 Time when the meeting closed.

The minutes are written in the minute-book and usually the pertinent documents are kept there too, for future reference.

The conduct of the meeting

The kind of meeting we are discussing is usually run along lines *similar* to, but not identical with Parliamentary procedure. This 'popular procedure', as it is sometimes called, is a vast subject and way beyond the scope of a book on etiquette. But what happens, very briefly, is this: once the preliminary formalities are over, the actual business of the meeting begins through the consideration of the motions put before it.

The bye-laws of many societies stipulate that all motions

should be submitted in writing to the secretary, seven, ten, or even twenty-one days before the meeting takes place. In such cases, the secretary puts them on the agenda and they are brought up in chronological order. There are cases, however, where motions are not put in writing, formal motions being one of these exceptions.

A motion must always be framed in the affirmative and must begin with the word 'That'.

A motion is put before the meeting by its proposer, who rises and states his case and then ends by repeating the actual words of his motion, beginning: 'That this, that or the other should be done. . . .'

Although it is not legally necessary to have a seconder for every motion, the standing orders or rules of most societies do require it. Having said his piece, either ending or beginning with the exact wording of his motion, the proposer sits down and, with a bit of luck, someone will then rise and second his motion, either simply by repeating the formula: 'I second the motion' or by making a brief speech in favour of the motion.

However, should no one be willing to second the motion, the chairman will wait for a while and then announce that the motion has failed, since it lacks a seconder. The subject is then closed and the same motion, either in its original or in a different form, cannot be raised again at the same meeting.

Let us assume, however, that the motion has been both proposed and seconded. It is now open for debate and anyone can rise and speak on it. No one may speak more than once on the same question, except the proposer of the motion, who is entitled to reply to criticisms made or to give explanations and amplifications. His reply, however, must close the debate on the question.

Inevitably, there will be dissident voices. Quite apart from those who are entirely against the motion, there will be those who think the motion is too sweeping in its extent, and those who, on the contrary, feel it does not go far enough. Others will feel that it could be worded more clearly or more forcefully or more in line with their own thinking on the subject. These dissenters will therefore want to suggest alterations to the motion. These alterations are called amendments.

Amendments, too, have their proper form. They should:

1 Leave out words.

2 Insert words.

3 Substitute some words for other words.

This does not mean, of course, that the word 'not' can be inserted in the strategic place in order to negate the whole motion. In other words, if the motion is 'That a new playground be built somewhere in the borough' it cannot be amended to read: 'That *no* new playground be built....' The time to show such total disapproval is voting time.

Like motions, amendments must be affirmative. They may be proposed by anyone, except the proposer and seconder of the motion. Amendments do not need a seconder by law, but it is the almost universal custom to require a seconder and, indeed the rules, standing orders, or other regulations of many bodies require it.

The seconder of an amendment may either make his speech in favour when he rises to second the amendment, or later on, but he may not make any further remark during the discussion which follows.

In the 'popular procedure' it is the general practice to vote on the amendment before voting on the motion which it seeks to amend. If the amendment is carried, the motion as amended will take the place of the original one.

Each amendment is treated in the same fashion until the subject is exhausted. Finally, the motion as a whole is put to the vote.

It is also possible to propose an amendment to an amendment but this cumbersome procedure tends to cloud the issue and confuse those present. The best way to handle such a situation is to forget about the original motion temporarily, consider the first amendment as the motion itself and the second amendment as an amendment to it. If the second amendment is carried, the first amendment is re-worded accordingly and this new version is then considered in connection with the original motion.

In Parliament and all political debating societies, the motion is voted on first and the amendments afterwards.

When the chairman feels that the question has been sufficiently discussed and everyone has been given an opportunity to have his say, he will ask the meeting whether they now wish the question to be voted upon. If he gets an affirmative reply he will call upon the mover of the motion to reply, after which he will rise and say: 'The question is that this assembly is of the opinion that...'. Having completed the question, he will pause and then add: 'All those in favour please say "Aye".' When the response has died down, he will add: 'All those against say "No".'

Having assessed the 'Ayes' and the 'Noes', the chairman will announce: 'I think the "Ayes" have it' or 'the "Noes"', as the case may be. If the chairman is not challenged, then the motion is carried. Otherwise, he will have to call for a show of hands. In such a case he usually appoints a teller for and one against, and when the votes have been counted he reads them out and announces the result of the voting accordingly.

It is not necessary to wait for the chairman to close the meeting. Anyone, in fact, can attempt to bring it to a close in a variety of ways. There are also a number of tactics which can be resorted to in order to avoid a vote being taken on a particular motion and all these intricacies can be studied in the many books published on the subject.

Committees

There are at least five kinds of committees:

1 The executive committee, which is responsible for the actual management of the organization.

2 The standing committee, a permanent committee set up annually to carry out administrative tasks of a particular kind.

3 The *ad hoc* or special committee, which, as the names imply, is set up for a special purpose and goes out of office when the purpose has been reached.

4 The joint committee, which is usually set up to co-ordinate the activities of two or more bodies.

5 The sub-committee, which perhaps does not deserve a heading of its own, since it is simply an off-shoot of another committee, usually formed to relieve its parent committee of some of its detail work.

Provided its limitations are understood, a properly constructed and well-run committee can serve a number of valuable purposes. Dr Copeman* lists no less than five:

1 To bring together for regular, formal liaison, colleagues whose co-ordination of activities might otherwise be difficult to achieve, or might go by default.

2 To pool ideas and experience in order to construct a common plan for action, to which all may be persuaded to agree, and in which all may feel that they are participating.

3 To obtain the considered views of members of the committee on a matter which is beyond the experience of one of them — usually the chairman. Any views which he obtains in committee are likely to be proffered more seriously and objectively than if offered privately, if only because they are subject to potential criticism by colleagues who may be present.

4 To exercise authority which is too great for one man if only because outside opinion can be better reassured that any decisions taken are wiser for having been taken collectively.

5 To diffuse responsibility among several executives, so that none may be held to have stood individually in judgment on his fellow-men.

The size of a committee will, of course, vary, but twenty is considered to be near the maximum useful number and five the smallest number, although the committee of one has been known to exist. The rule-of-thumb should be to keep the number down as much as consistent with usefulness.

The size of the committee will determine what is to constitute a quorum. Three is the lowest number practicable, although

* *Laws of Business Management and the Executive Way of Life.* George Copeman, Business Publications Limited, Second Edition, 1963.

with small committees it is often decided that all members must always be present.

In business concerns, the highest-ranking executive usually takes the chair, although committees frequently nominate their chairman in much the same way as general meetings do.

Committee procedure is far less formal than the 'popular procedure' previously described. Members usually sit around a table and discuss the problems before them much as in an ordinary business meeting.

Behaviour at a meeting has already been discussed in Chapter 3 and much of what was said there holds good for the committee meeting.

Minutes are also kept at committee meetings and, in the case of business companies, they are frequently used as a report to top management on the committee's progress. While this is an excellent opportunity for top management to be made aware of committee members' problems and attitudes, great care must be exercised in reporting such things so as not to bring discredit on any of the members. Obviously, if any executive found himself put in a false light, he would no longer express himself with such freedom and one of the main objectives of the meetings would be lost.

Likewise, an executive should be very careful not to criticize a colleague personally at a meeting. If he needs to bring up something about a colleague's department, then he should ask the colleague to be present. In this way, both sides of the story can be heard and will be reflected in the minutes. In any event, it is always wise to criticize policies and their result, rather than personalities.

In the case of a committee of a society or other body, once the problem has been thoroughly thrashed out, a report is prepared for submission to the full society. First of all, a rough draft of the report is written and then a day is set aside to go over it, paragraph by paragraph. Each section is treated as a motion subject to amendments and is voted upon. Finally, a vote is taken to submit the report to the full body, who then considers it and decides what action is to be taken.

Unfortunately, it is said that no more than 50 per cent of reports are accepted in their entirety, although some are adopted with modifications.

chapter thirteen

clubs

Like the tea-break, clubs are a British invention. To the super-
ficial observer, the *raison d'être* of a club appears perfectly simple
and crystal clear – to bring together like-minded people for the
pursuit of common interests. Closer investigation, however, brings
to light the fact that clubs exist for a variety of other reasons.

Theatre clubs seem to exist to enable their members to view
plays which the Lord Chamberlain has not passed or would not
pass. Film clubs seem to serve the same purpose for films. Dance
clubs obviously serve the purpose of circumventing the Sunday
Observance Act. At least some businessmen's luncheon clubs
seem to exist to enable members to eat in the company of their
peers, well away from the common herd. As for the traditional
English clubs, it is really quite hard to discover what purpose
they *do* serve, since some of them sound so cold, uncomfortable,
and lonely. When asked the question bluntly, the secretary of
one very famous club replied that its purpose was to enable
members to get away from people. Indeed, according to Anthony
Sampson,* members of some clubs are virtually forbidden to
talk to a member they do not know – unless properly introduced,
no doubt. Persistent investigation and inquiry do confirm the

* *Anatomy of Britain Today.* Hodder and Stoughton, 1965.

L

fact that the traditional British club represents for its members an oasis of peace and quiet in familiar surroundings. It is a refuge from the harassments of the outside world, a home from home for the out-of-town member, and a safe forwarding address.

It follows from the above that before attempting to join a club

'. . . unless properly introduced'

of any sort, you would be well advised to make sure it is the kind of club you want to join. Not all the famous clubs are unsociable, of course. The Savage and the Garrick, for instance, are very friendly.

Strange things happen when the sociable and the unsociable clubs meet on each other's ground. This usually happens once a year, when it is customary for one club to grant hospitality to another during its annual closure. Members of the Travellers' Club frequently 'discover' each other for the first time during their annual visit to the Garrick, where conversation between members is encouraged. Certainly such a state of affairs could only exist in Britain.

Having made quite sure that the club you propose to join is your cup of tea, the next step is to gain admission. With theatre clubs and the like, as well as a great number of luncheon clubs, joining is simply a question of paying a small fee, signing a membership card, and perhaps waiting a day or two before you get it. It is now even possible to join over 200 dining and wining clubs across the country at one fell swoop for an annual subscription of six guineas.

To join the more exclusive clubs, however, you have to be eligible for membership, first of all, and then to have a proposer and a seconder. Some of the famous clubs still have the same requirements as when they were founded over a hundred years ago and they make quaint reading. To qualify for membership of the Reform Club, for instance, you must subscribe to the Reform Bill of 1832. To join the Travellers' Club, you must have travelled at least 500 miles from London outside the British Isles.

Yet for all their aura of exclusiveness and mystery, clubs, in practice, welcome almost any new member and very few of them have a waiting list. Only a few have black balls.

A club's rules often require the name of the candidate, together with those of his proposer and seconder, to be exhibited on a notice-board on the club premises for a specified length of time. Other clubs have a nomination form which has to be filled in by the candidate for membership. The rules may call for election by the club's general committee or by a special membership committee or sub-committee.

The entrance fee and first subscription become payable when you are notified of your election.

As a fledgeling club member, you will be expected to pay your subscription regularly, respect club property, and observe the rules of the club. Some of the rules are unwritten, so it will pay you to act as if you had entered a foreign country, listening and observing before acting. As already mentioned, some clubs are places to get away from people, rather than to meet people. In such clubs you will keep yourself to yourself, which will probably be the reason for your joining. Obviously, such an unsociable club is the last place for a businessman aiming at meeting prospective clients. In fact, some clubs actually forbid members to produce business documents, which is another reason why the businessman will want to investigate a club thoroughly before joining.

Resigning from a club is far simpler than joining. Unless the club rules provide otherwise, all you need do when you have had enough is to write a letter of resignation to the club secretary or proprietor. There is no need for him or anyone else formally to accept your resignation. You have resigned and that is that.

chapter fourteen

women in business

There is no reason at all why dealing with women executives should present a problem. Since time immemorial, however, man has conditioned himself and everybody else to think of woman as an inferior being and is consequently liable to find himself thrown off balance when he comes face to face with the woman executive – capable, well-informed, efficient, and poised. He cannot quite believe his eyes and, nine times out of ten, insists on treating her with condescension or avoids dealing with her at all, if he can possibly help it.

The golden rule to bear in mind is that, basically, there are no men and women in business, but just people with a job of work to do. In fact, just as personalities should be left out of business, so should sex. So forget you are dealing with a woman and deal instead with the sales director, the editor, or the consultant, as the case may be.

This does not mean, of course, that you should treat the woman executive just like another man, slap her on the back and take her to the local for a pint. She *will* appreciate the normal courtesies that you reserve for women, but far more important to her is to be treated like a person with a job of work to do. In point of fact, women are tremendously adaptable creatures and will adjust quite happily to bad language, snatching a sandwich in a pub, and most of the other rough and ready male ways. She does not like to feel she is inhibiting her male colleagues and will go more than half way towards meeting you. If you can see your way to doing the same for her, she will greatly appreciate it.

She will not mind your calling her by her Christian name, providing you know her well enough and you expect her to reciprocate. One young male executive once exclaimed as he read a letter: 'Good gracious, she calls me John.' It had apparently slipped his mind that he had spent most of the previous afternoon calling her Jane and quite obviously expected her to call him 'Mister', although they were of similar level and age group. Male arrogance is not good manners.

Give her credit for objectivity, fairness, and business sense. If she lacked these qualities, she would not be in her present position. Obviously, if she is a creative person, and many women executives are, then she will behave like one, rather than like a person from the City.

Some women executives spend a great deal of time doing for others things that men normally do for them, such as ordering meals, organizing transport, dealing with waiters, porters, and other staff. Consequently, there is no greater luxury for them than to be able to relax when away from business and let a thoughtful man take care of all these details for them.

Hints for the woman executive

The way up the executive ladder is an arduous one indeed for a woman. She can expect male prejudice, obstructionism, and envy to dog her footsteps every inch of the way. Only the most persistent, capable, and determined women can hope to reach even mid-way up the ladder. Once they have gone that far, however, they certainly do not need any hints on how to behave, for they inevitably possess all the tact, diplomacy, and *savoir faire* in the world. Without these qualities, they would never have made the grade. These hints are, therefore, offered in all humility to the up and coming young women executives and to those who aspire to take up this most gruelling of challenges.

The woman executive's prime concern should be to get on with the job, not to parade her femininity. She should not constantly remind her male colleagues, customers or others, that she is a woman by wearing provocative clothes, theatrical make-up or heady perfume. She should use logic and persuasion to get her points across, not feminine wiles. Cattiness, sexy innuendoes, tantrums, and tears should all be strictly taboo.

The woman executive should strive always to be businesslike, objective, and firm when necessary. It is far more important for a woman to be firm than a man, since so many people, including subordinates, are inclined to try to take advantage of a woman, whereas they would not dream of trying it on a man.

All of this does not mean that a woman executive should act tough and ape men. Nothing could be more unattractive or more unnecessary. On the contrary, she would do well to remember the saying: 'Softly, softly catchee monkey.'

As for signing letters, a woman should sign Mary Brown or Joan Smith. She should not feel the need to hide behind her initials. To help her correspondents, she can then add 'Miss' or 'Mrs' after the typewritten name. Some married women continue to call themselves 'Miss' in business, but there is no firm ruling about this. It is entirely a matter of choice and there are probably about as many married businesswomen who call themselves 'Miss' as 'Mrs'. The most common practice, apart from the 'handle', is for married women to use their own Christian name followed by their husband's surname. In fact it would not be at all surprising to see the custom of married women using their husband's Christian name and surname dying out all together.

When entertaining a man in a restaurant, the diplomatic businesswoman will make arrangements before so that the bill is paid by post. The most tactful women of all make sure that the bill does not even appear for them to sign, thus sparing their male guests even the faintest hint of embarrassment.

The tactful businesswoman will either enlist her male guest's help in choosing the wine or leave the choice entirely to him, even if her own knowledge and experience are far greater than his.

If the married woman executive's domestic life is unhappy it will inevitably be reflected in her work. It is, therefore, extremely important for her to dovetail the two facets of her life successfully. One eminently successful woman in both spheres has been guided by three rules:

1 Get home at the same time as your husband, or preferably five minutes before him.

2 Take your holidays with him.

3 Don't be mysterious about the people you meet. On the contrary, if you mention the subject at all, be open and specific about it. For instance, you might say: 'I met Bill Smith for lunch today and we discussed the new agency we're trying to set up in France.'

The idea here is to reassure him, rather than to tease him and make him wonder what you get up to when you lunch with all those fascinating men.

The woman executive will obviously be every bit as careful about her dress and grooming as her male counterpart. How she will dress will rather depend on what business she is in. If she is in fashion or one of the other 'glamour' fields, she will no doubt follow fashion closely, but otherwise she will perhaps feel that an elegant, somewhat conservative style will be more suitable.

The woman executive should not wear loud, eccentric or very *avant-garde* clothes, any more than her male counterpart should. She should certainly not blend in with the wallpaper, but neither should her appearance constantly call attention to the fact that she is a woman. It is grossly unfair to be constantly twining and untwining a pair of shapely legs before the men's eyes or to keep putting them off their stroke with a daring *décolleté*.

By not calling attention to herself as a woman she will stand a far greater chance of being accepted on her merits and for the qualities she brings to her job.

For speaking engagements, it is even more important to be well turned out, as we have seen in Chapter 11. Red is not a good colour for such an occasion, since it is inclined to strain the eyesight – and you do want to keep your audience's eyes on you. Your hat should be smart, but not eccentric, for you do not want your audience to be so fascinated by your hat that they do not listen to what you are saying.

And this brings us back to the most vital point of all: a businesswoman's dress should be secondary to her. Her functions are more important than her fashion.

chapter fifteen

the businessman abroad

When you travel abroad you automatically become one of Britain's unofficial ambassadors-at-large. Everything you do will reflect upon Britons in general. The reason why Americans, Germans, Italians, or any other nationality have a bad reputation for this or that is not that all Americans or Germans have those particular traits, but that a handful of people have cast a slur upon their nation by boorish behaviour. Two ill-mannered and inconsiderate travellers will stand out a mile; ten perfectly well-behaved travellers will go unnoticed.

The moral is, of course, that it is even more important to be polite at all times when travelling abroad than it is at home. Some details of etiquette may vary in some countries, but good manners are a world-wide currency. No one will take it amiss if you slip up on a minor point of etiquette, providing you display innate good manners and are friendly and modest, rather than haughty and standoffish.

The businessman travelling abroad could do nothing better than:

1 Learn at least a smattering of the language of the country he plans to visit. It is flattering to the host country to know

that the visitor has at least made the effort. The arrogant 'Let them learn English' days are over.

2 Practice his smile. A smile is an international language. It can open doors and win friends for you without your uttering a word.

3 Learn how to bow. There is no reason to panic. A slight bow from the waist is not really so theatrical and there is no reason at all why an Englishman should not learn this small courtesy which is useful in many Continental countries, and especially in the Far East.

Whether travelling by car, train, 'plane or ship it simply boils down to following regulations and being considerate to your fellow-travellers, pedestrians or other drivers, as the case may be.

Road signs are gradually being internationalized, but you would still be well advised to arm yourself with a copy of the local driving regulations, if you are not given one at the frontier. More than good manners may be involved, particularly in view of the more aggressive Continental driving habits.

In trains, you will obviously refrain from smoking in a non-smoker, consider your fellow-passengers in the matter of having windows and blinds up or down, you will occupy only your allotted space, and you will help women-passengers or elderly people put their suitcases up on the rack if you see they are without a porter.

Travellers on the Continent and almost anywhere, in fact, are somewhat less reserved than we are in Britain, and if you do not respond to a friendly question or remark you will be considered cold and uncongenial. The ideal solution to the question of how much to talk to one's fellow passengers really boils down to finding the golden mean: be friendly and responsive without intruding too heavily. If you are particularly keen to finish your *Financial Times*, no one will stop you, but *do* attempt to smile and appear approachable at some stage.

In 'planes, you will have very few problems of etiquette. You will take your seat and sit there most of the time, so all you will need to worry about is to follow instructions about when to put your cigarette out, when to fasten your seat belt, and, of course, not to be too demanding of the stewardess.

On board ship, rather more is involved, since a voyage is usually far longer than other journeys and passengers are in close proximity often for several days. It is, therefore, very important to know your way about and to be considerate both of your fellow-passengers and of the ship's officers and crew with whom you come in contact.

The *purser* will want your passport and will take care of your valuables, deal with any complaints about your cabin, book you for shore excursions, sell you foreign currency, or cash your travellers cheques, except in some of the larger ships where there is a cashier.

The *chief dining-room steward* takes care of seating arrangements in the dining-room and you should see him if you have any preferences as to where you want to sit or with regard to taking first or second sitting for meals. Indeed, if you happen to be travelling 'Tourist' on a large liner and feel very strongly about which sitting you prefer, you had better see the chief dining-room steward as soon as you possibly can or you will be disappointed.

The *deck steward* is another who will contribute greatly to your comfort. He is in charge of the deck chairs and deck games and you should see him as soon as possible if you are keen to have your deck chair on the lee side or other preferred spot. A word with the deck steward and your deck chair will be in your selected spot all ready for you every morning – for a small fee, of course.

Some ships have *cabin stewards* and *stewardesses* and some have either one or the other. But whatever their sex, cabin stewards keep your cabin clean, make your bed, bring you breakfast in bed, if you want it, have your luggage brought up from the luggage-room or check for you if it hasn't arrived in your cabin and so on.

Marking your luggage is very important on a sea voyage, for if you do not do it correctly you will find yourself without the clothes you need. Any luggage not wanted during the voyage should be marked 'Not Wanted on Voyage'. It will then go into the hold and you will not see it again until you land. All the luggage that you *do* need should be marked 'Wanted on Voyage'. Obviously, you would do well to keep the pieces as few as possible, since space is limited in most cabins. On longer voyages, some of the 'wanted' luggage goes into the luggage-room and you can send for it when you want it. All these details are explained to you by the shipping line and appropriate labels supplied, so there is no reason why you should go wrong.

Life on board ship is quite informal and free and easy and you can certainly speak to anyone without a formal introduction. In the first class, passengers change for dinner, except on the first and last nights of the voyage. In other classes, most men wear lounge suits for dinner and women dress up a little. On gala occasions, some men like to wear dinner jackets, irrespective of the class in which they are travelling. At lunchtime, most passengers dress quite informally, but just *how* informally depends to a certain extent on the ship and its flag. When in doubt, there is no harm in asking your dining-room steward or, if you are very cautious indeed, being slightly less daring the first day and noticing what other passengers do. This is a very useful expedient which will serve you in good stead wherever you go abroad.

Tipping

One of the biggest bugbears of travel is the question of tipping. To make matters worse, no two 'experts' agree on what is the 'right' tip for a given situation. So, to add to the confusion, here are a few more tips on tipping:

Railway porters: In Britain, tip 1s if you have only one case or 9d for each case if you have more than one. A trunk calls for 1s 6d to 2s. Give him an extra shilling if he finds you a special seat as well. In the u.s.a., the official rate is 25 cents for each piece of baggage, but the porter usually expects a little extra. In most countries on the Continent there is a fixed tariff and it is usually posted in railway stations. If there is no clue, then tip the same as you would at home.

Porters at airports: In Britain, it is not customary to tip airline porters. In the u.s.a., the rate is the same as for railway porters and likewise on the Continent.

Porters at seaports: The same as for other porters.

Sleeping-car attendant: Half-a-crown in Britain, 50 cents to a dollar in the U.S.A., and on the Continent roughly as in Britain.

Restaurant car: A service charge will usually be included in the bill. If it is not, then leave a tip equal to about 12½ per cent of the total. Airline stewards and hostesses are not tipped. In fact, air travel is the least tip-riddled form of travel.

On board ship: The 'experts' are at great variance as to the size of the correct tip, all of which proves that it is largely up to you. If you can afford it and were well taken care of, you can be as generous as you like. The P. & O. Line publish a leaflet on the subject and if you are travelling by their ships you may well decide to follow their advice. Other steamship lines feel that the way to arrive at the correct tip is to allot a percentage of the fare to tips. The Cunard Steamship Company feel that between 5 and 7 per cent of the fare is an accepted standard, another line suggests 7½ per cent as a minimum, while some people are known to ear-mark 10 per cent of the fare to tips, which is what Emily Post recommends.* Yet another way to solve the problem is to ask the purser's advice. It is true that some of them will tell you it is as you please, but others will oblige you with a list of suggestions.

Once you have settled on the lump sum to allot to tips, you have to decide how to divide it. The usually accepted practice is to give a sum equal to slightly less than half the total to both the cabin steward and the dining-room steward and distribute the remainder to others who have been of service to you. The wine steward and the barman are tipped as and when they serve you.

It should not be necessary to add that the ship's officers are never tipped. On the other hand, it is courteous to thank the purser for his help and kindness before you disembark, as well as any other officer with whom you have become friendly or who has been helpful.

At hotels and in restaurants: The custom of adding a service charge to hotel and restaurant bills is now almost universal. If you have any doubt as to whether the service is included, ask. If service is not included, then tip between 10 and 15 per cent

* *Emily Post's Etiquette*. Revised by Elizabeth L. Post, Funk & Wagnalls, Inc., New York, Eleventh Edition, 1965.

of the bill, whether for a stay in a hotel or for a meal in a restaurant. Unfortunately, in many countries, including Britain, it is customary to leave a small tip even though the gratuity has already been included in the bill. This seems rather an imposition on top of 15 per cent, but some hotel porters are known to become quite unco-operative with a guest who is known not to have left an additional tip. In France, it is usual to tip the wine waiter in first-class restaurants, while in Britain it is customary to tip the carver in the type of restaurant where he wheels the joint up to your table and carves it in front of you. In the U.S.A. the 'Captain', i.e. the head waiter, will expect $1 or $2, according to the size of your party.

If the tipping at your hotel is left to you, then slightly less than half the allotted amount should go to the dining-room waiter and a like sum divided between the chambermaid and the porters. If you have only breakfast in the hotel, then the waiter should obviously get a smaller tip. Porters and pages are tipped when they do something for you, porters getting between 1s 6d and 2s 6d for two cases and pages 6d or a 1s according to the errand and the type of hotel. Floor waiters are tipped either when they render the service or at the end of your stay. The same applies to the barman, who gets 10 to 12 per cent of your drinks bill. The lounge waiter will expect 6d or 1s and the doorman will expect the same for getting you a taxi. It is not, strictly speaking, necessary to tip the head waiter or the head porter unless they have done something special for you. If you *do*, then you can hardly give them less than 10s in view of their exalted position.

Theatres and cinemas: It is customary to tip theatre and cinema usherettes in France, Italy, Portugal, Belgium, and Spain. It is not customary in Greece, Denmark, Switzerland, Norway, Sweden, Austria, Germany, and Finland. In Holland, it is optional.

Taxis: Taxi drivers in Britain are beginning to consider 6d too small a tip however short the drive. On a 4s fare, 1s is considered to be the smallest possible tip. After that you can add 3d for every shilling shown on the meter, plus 6d. Certainly, if the taxi driver has been particularly helpful, has had to wait for you or hurry to enable you to catch a train, then you will, no doubt, be only too pleased to reward him with a larger tip.

In Norway, Finland, and behind the Iron Curtain, taxi drivers do not expect a tip. In Germany, they expect small change only. In Yugoslavia and Spain, give no more than 10 per cent of the fare. In the u.s.a., a quarter (25 cents) is the minimum, with corresponding increases roughly as in Britain. Elsewhere, tip as in Britain.

At garages: A small tip is expected in most Continental countries except Denmark, Norway, Sweden, Holland, and Finland.

ON THE CONTINENT

Cold. Reserved. Phlegmatic. These are the adjectives used all over the Continent to describe the Englishman. Certainly, if you want to win friends and customers, you should do all you can to dispel this triple verdict. Perhaps it should be added in all fairness that Britons are also considered to be 'correct', punctual, and reliable. In fact, Spaniards frequently mention *la punctualidad inglesa* and marvel at it, as at some awe-inspiring virtue.

Some customs are common throughout the Continent and a familiarity with them will enable you to to maintain the British reputation for 'correctness' wherever you go. While the correct sizes for business and private cards vary from country to country, you obviously would not be expected to have a different size for each country you visit. You would, however, find it useful to know the Continental abbreviations which are used to send a message with a visiting-card. The following initials are written in the lower left-hand corner of the card:

p.c.	*pour condoler* ⎫	either of these can be used to
p.p.p.	*pour prendre part* ⎭	send condolences
p.f.	*pour féliciter*	to congratulate
p.p.	*pour présenter*	to introduce
p.f.n.a.	*pour féliciter nouvel an*	to wish a Happy New Year
p.p.c.	*pour prendre congé*	to say good-bye
p.r.	*pour remercier*	to thank

If you receive a card marked: 'p.c.', 'p.p.p.', or 'p.f.' you should immediately send one back marked 'p.r.' A card marked 'p.r.' is also sent with flowers or chocolates to your hostess after you have been entertained.

Should you receive a card marked 'p.f.n.a.', send one back promptly marked in the same way. This may, or may not, convince the sender that you thought of him at about the same time. If he was rather late, however, you will not get away with it and there will be nothing for it but to reply with a card initialled 'p.r.p.f.' meaning 'Thank you for your good wishes and the same to you.'

Cards marked 'p.p.' are used to introduce others, not yourself. If you wish to introduce a colleague or business friend visiting another town, you can give him your card marked 'p.p.' which he will add to his own and send off in an envelope to the person to whom you are introducing him. He will then follow this up with a personal visit. On no account should the 'p.p.' card be presented personally.

Cards marked 'p.p', 'p.p.c.', and 'p.r.' do not call for a reply.

Another custom which is being revived all over the Continent is handkissing. In Germany and Italy it had fallen into disfavour during their respective dictatorships and, indeed, even handshaking was discouraged by Mussolini, but now the handkiss is all the rage again and the ladies seem to like it very much. In fact, some of them all but force you to kiss their hand by giving it to you palm downwards. This is, of course, bad manners on a woman's part, but should it happen to you on your next trip to the Continent, there will be nothing for it but to comply. How will you acquit yourself?

The technique is simple enough, once you know how. You do not yank the lady's hand up to your lips, but you bend over her hand, stopping short just before your lips touch the back of her hand. In other words, you do not kiss her hand at all, but bend over it. The Italians do indeed go all the way, as it were, but in Italy, too, the so-called German version, which stops short just before reaching the hand, is recognized and preferred by some men. The illustration on page 167 shows you exactly how to do it.

Apart from the technique, there are one or two points to be borne in mind on this matter of handkissing:

1 Only married women, or elderly or distinguished single

women, are entitled to the handkiss. It is a mark of respect, not a declaration of love.

The Handkiss

2 Handkissing belongs indoors only. The only exception to this rule is the garden party, where hands may be kissed. The reason for this exception is that a private garden is considered to all intents and purposes to be part of the home.

3 It is perfectly in order to bow over a gloved hand. If, however, you are in Italy, the lady is especially attractive and you feel like casting aside your British reserve and really kissing

M

her hand, then, alas, you will have to refrain if she is wearing gloves. Italian etiquette books say that it is very bad form to seek out a spot which the glove does *not* cover, but a British businessman hardly needs such an admonition.

Not *all* Continental countries go in for handkissing. They do not do it much in Switzerland, for instance, but it is said to be very popular in Bosnia! It is easy enough to take your cue from the other men, however, and in all probability few British men would dare to try their hand at it anyway. But such are the rules, for the record.

You will not find the quaint British custom of the women leaving the men to their port after dinner on the Continent, so be prepared to have your coffee at the dinner-table or to move to the living-room for it. Moreover, only in Britain does the man wait for the woman to greet him in the street. If you meet a woman you know, either on the Continent, or anywhere else in the world, it is up to you to raise your hat, if you are wearing one, and to bow to her.

You will find that all women on the Continent and elsewhere give you their hand when you are introduced, so be prepared for it.

You will also find that, in Germany and Scandinavian countries, host and hostess do not take the head and foot of the table, as in Britain, but sit half way down the long side of the table, facing one another. The head and foot are reserved for the two least important guests. This would not affect you, as a guest, of course, but it is just as well to know what to expect. Seating arrangements also vary in some countries, although most Continental countries, as well as the u.s.a., use the same seating arrangements as we do, this being an international custom. In Germany and in Scandinavian countries, it is the other way round, i.e. the most important male guest sits on the hostess's *left*, the most important lady on the host's *left* and so on. When foreign guests are present, however, German and Scandinavian hosts sometimes use the international seating arrangement in their honour. So be prepared for anything and watch the place-cards.

As far as table manners are concerned, it is more a question of suffering alien table manners gladly. Perhaps no one, or hardly anyone, eats as neatly, or indeed as unenthusiastically, as the British, and consequently you may find the noisy soup-eaters and napkin-around-neck tuckers abroad rather hard to take. You will have to bear up, of course, but you will not be expected to follow suit. Sometimes the very civilized British way of eating inhibits people. Spaniards, for instance, often appear embarrassed if you daintily cut your chicken with knife and fork and feel that you are standing unnecessarily on ceremony. It is up to you to use your sixth sense in such cases and to follow your hosts' example if you feel it would help. This is a case when good manners take precedence over etiquette. When abroad, you would do well to bear this maxim in mind always. It is not so much your own idea of etiquette which counts, but rather consideration for others. You should aim not merely to feel at home with all people, but also to make all people feel at home with you – and this is rather harder to achieve.

Germany

Germany is perhaps the country whose social customs and rules of behaviour are most closely akin to our own.

Germans, very much including businessmen, are keen on titles and it is customary to call everyone by his job title or other title. The managing director of a company will be called *Herr General Direktor* or *Herr Direktor,* as the case may be, even socially. In smaller towns, everyone from the mayor down will be addressed by his title: *Herr Bürgermeister, Herr Doktor, Herr Apotheker, Herr Lehrer,* and so on. Even the wives take on the title of their husband, although this is now old-fashioned and not strictly correct. You should, therefore, keep your ears alert for people's titles and use them until modestly invited to drop the title.

Introductions follow the same rules as in Britain, the only difference being that, as already mentioned, you should be prepared for ladies to give you their hand. You may then bow over it if you wish. According to the distinguished German experts on the subject, Karheinz Graudenz and Erika Pappritz,* you should not say anything when being introduced to someone, but

* *Etikette Neu.* Karheinz Graudenz and Erika Pappritz, Südwest Verlag, Munich.

M*

simply smile and bow and then carry on with the conversation. In practice, however, you will find that 90 per cent of Germans say either *'Sehr angenehm'* or *Sehr erfreut'*. If you speak not a word of German, you will therefore be perfectly 'correct' if you merely bow, smile, and shake hands.

German businessmen do as much business entertaining in their homes as we do in Britain, but you will find very few stumbling blocks here. German table manners are very much the same as ours, but strangely enough, it is considered 'barbaric – no less – to cut potatoes with a knife. As an Englishman, however, you would not be expected to alter your customary table manners.

Do not begin to drink until your host raises his glass. This is, as it were, the green light for drinking to begin. A German seldom, if ever, drinks without raising his glass first to his part-ner, then to his hostess and the next time around to one of the other ladies. At an all-male dinner, you raise your glass to some-one at your own level or of higher rank. If someone raises his glass to you, then you must reciprocate later on, but do not delay too long. Glasses are clinked only when wine or champagne is drunk.

In Germany, cigarettes are passed around after the roast. Coffee is taken either at the table or in the living-room and the sexes are not segregated.

While there are no hard and fast rules about it, it is perhaps more customary in Germany than in England to send flowers to your hostess. They may either be sent ahead of you, in which case they should arrive about two hours before you, or afterwards, in which case they should arrive no later than noon the following day.

France

André Maurois once said that the Americans are democratic in that they call everyone 'Joe' or 'Jill', from the boss to the boot-black, while the French are democratic in that they call everyone *Monsieur,* from *Monsieur le Président de la République* to *Monsieur le Concierge.* This is roughly correct and the lesson is that in France you should address people as *Monsieur, Madame* or *Mademoiselle,* as the case may be. There is not

the German keenness for titles, but the formality of *Monsieur*
for everyone, however humble. But never add the surname,
unless you are addressing someone of much lower rank.

The formalities of introductions are the same as in Britain,
but it is not done to ask for the name to be repeated if you did
not catch it. This offends the Frenchman's pride, who feels that
you *should* have caught it! As you shake hands, you need only
murmur '*Monsieur*', '*Madame*', or '*Mademoiselle*', but you will
find that the great majority of Frenchmen say '*Enchanté,
Monsieur*'. Introductions aside, you will do a lot of handshaking
while in France, since Frenchmen shake hands all around every
time they arrive and leave, and this includes coming and going
to the office. Just about everyone is included, even the *patron* at
the *bistro* and the waiter.

A good deal of business entertaining is done, frequently in
hotels and restaurants, but sometimes also at home. After a
dinner invitation to someone's home, send a few words of thanks
to the hostess. Flowers are not sent until you have got to know the
couple better. If you share a table in a restaurant, you are not
expected to get into conversation with the other occupants of the
table. When you leave, however, you are expected to bow slightly
and murmur '*Monsieur*', '*Messieurs*', or as the case may be. You
will find that the waiter will bring your bill before you have
finished your meal. This is customary in France and does not
mean the waiter is anxious to get rid of you.

The French are extremely polite people and while in France
you cannot do better than to follow the French dictum '*Toujours
la politesse*'.

Spain

The most outstanding characteristic of the Spaniard is his pride,
and if you will remember to do nothing that could in any way
offend it, you will get on well in Spain. To his pride the Spaniard
adds dignity and graciousness. Your behaviour in Spain should
therefore be modelled on these three Spanish characteristics.
Even the most humble woman should be addressed as *Señora*
until you know her name, when she will become *Doña Maria,
Doña Encarnaciòn* or whatever her Christian name may be.

Even the top executive of a company is *Don José* or *Don Pedro* to his employees, so keep your ear tuned so that you too can use the same form of address as others. Spaniards who travel abroad a lot endeavour to adopt the general custom of calling a man Mr (Surname), but the true Spanish fashion is *Don* (Christian name).

Letters of recommendation are especially useful in Spain and you will also do well to be well supplied with business cards. Introductions follow the same rules as elsewhere and most Spaniards say *'Mucho gusto!'* for 'How do you do?'

Spaniards are quite formal dressers and you will seldom, if ever, have occasion to go out without a jacket and tie. If your wife is accompanying you, she should be very conservative in the way she dresses, because it is all too easy to offend by committing an 'indecency' in dress. Although bikinis are worn on some Spanish beaches, the best policy is to tread softly and look before unveiling legs, arms, and bosoms. If your wife is planning to visit churches or convents, she should not only wear a hat or a veil, but be sure to wear stockings, a dress with at least a short sleeve, a discreet neckline and a dress which covers her knees. Obviously, shorts for either men or women are out both in churches and in the streets.

Business entertaining in Spain is done mostly in cafés and indeed a great deal of business is talked over there, so you may never see the inside of a Spaniard's home. If this *should* happen, however, be sure to send along either flowers or chocolates as a 'Thank you' gesture. Otherwise, you would be well advised to steer clear of women. Spanish customs are still pretty old-fashioned and nothing could be easier than unwittingly to get into hot water over a woman. It is not done, for instance, for a man to invite a woman to lunch. If he does, the implication is that he expects something more to follow. The concept of friendship between a man and a woman just does not seem to exist in Spain. A man is either 'seriously' interested in a woman or else he has 'dishonourable' intentions and there are no half measures. Admittedly, things have been slowly changing during the past ten years or so, but old customs die hard and caution will be your best policy.

You will probably find Spanish hours rather hard to take. Office hours in the hotter parts of Spain used to change winter and summer, summer hours being from about 7 a.m. to 3 p.m., but this varies a great deal, with some offices following the English custom of having only one hour for lunch and finishing at 5.30 p.m. or so. Mealtimes are very much later than anywhere in the world, dinner seldom being served until 9.30 p.m. or 10 p.m. Spanish unpunctuality is also rather hard to take and something to which you will have to adjust yourself.

Two final tips: do not criticize the bullfight, the Spanish national 'sport', and be very careful with tipping. If there is no service charge on your hotel or restaurant bill, you will of course tip the usual 12 to 15 per cent. Railway porters we have already dealt with. Shoeshine-boys and page-boys obviously get tipped, but be very careful about tipping anyone else. If a boy or an old man shows you the way in the street, he does not expect a tip. It is his duty and his pleasure to be courteous to strangers. In Spain, even a beggar is dismissed with the words *'Vaya Vd. con Diós'* – 'Go with God'.

Italy

An Italian poet, Bonvesin de la Riva, wrote a lengthy poem on table manners as far back as the thirteenth century and the rules he laid down then are identical with those we follow to this day in Britain. When you visit Italy you may well have cause to notice that the Italians woefully neglect their thirteenth-century poets, but it may reassure you to know that you are probably following Signor de la Riva to the letter!

In any event, business entertaining is not so widespread in Italy as it is in Britain and you may or may not be entertained in the home. If you are, you will notice that many of the tasks which are performed in Britain by the host are taken over by the hostess in Italy. Otherwise, very formal dinners are much the same as in Britain, with both sexes taking coffee and liqueurs together either in the living-room or at the dinner-table. There is no smoking until the meal is over and the host has set the example. Italian hostesses appreciate flowers or chocolates.

In Italy you once again come up against that passion for titles which we first met in Germany. Even a minor acadamic degree, such as *Ragioniere,* which is less than a B.A., is tacked on before

ETIQUETTE FOR THE BUSINESSMAN

::

174   ETIQUETTE FOR THE BUSINESSMAN

the name and used on business cards, letter-heads, and in conversation. If a man has no academic title, then he certainly has a job title, a civic honour or perhaps even a title of nobility, despite the fact that Italy is a Republic. Consequently, your Italian business connections will probably be *Signor Direttore*, *Signor Avvocato* (if he is a lawyer), *Signor Dottore* (if he has a doctorate of any sort), *Signore Ragioniere* (if he is an accountant); or *Cavaliere* or *Commendatore* if he has a civil honour; or even a *Marchese* or a *Principe* – there are many of the latter in the fashion trade. You should therefore keep your ears open to catch the appropriate title. So widespread is this use of titles in Italy that people often call each other *Maestro, Professore* or any other title just for fun. Once you become acquainted with the person, you address him by his title alone, leaving out the Signor and his surname. Officers in the armed services are likewise addressed by the rank only, i.e. *Capitano, Tenente, Comandante*, and so on.

The formalities of introductions are the same as in Britain, except that Italians do not stand very much on ceremony, they introduce themselves or simply speak to people without having been introduced. The now obsolescent British custom of not speaking to anyone unless he has been properly introduced strikes the Italian as quite comical. When introduced, Italians usually say '*Piacere*', the most pedestrian expression, or '*Molto lieto*', '*Ben lieto*', '*Lietissimo*' or some such expression, or even '*Onorato*' if meeting a lady or a very important man.

Women take a back seat in Italy and it is not likely that you will see much of your Italian business connections' womenfolk. If you have an observant eye, you will notice that Italian men make a big show of being complimentary to women, but do not bother to relieve them of parcels, open doors for them, or show them very much consideration of any kind. A very recent Italian book of etiquette even goes so far as to say that it is no longer necessary for a man to escort a woman home after an evening out, since nowadays a woman is perfectly able to take care of herself.*

As in Spain, and indeed all Catholic countries, you should remind your wife to wear stockings and sleeves in church, as

* *Il Codice della Cortesia Italiana.* G. Bortone, Società Editrice Internazionale, Turin, 1966.

well as a hat or veil. If granted an audience by the Pope, women should wear a black dress with a high neckline and a black veil. A church should not be treated as a museum. It is very inconsiderate to wander around admiring the works of art while Mass is in progress. If you chance to go into a church while any religious ceremony is under way, good manners dictate that you stand, sit, or kneel discreetly in the background until it is over – and, of course, that you remove your hat. In Italian churches you may find that the singing or chanting of the congregation is well worth staying for.

All in all, if you unbend a little and do all you can do to be warm and friendly, you will have no difficulties in Italy.

IN THE U. S. A.

The only difficulty you are likely to experience in the U.S.A. is to be thought cold, excessively reserved, and formal. Any effort you can make to unbend, to smile, to take an interest in your fellow-men, to shed some of your formality will pay handsome dividends.

Americans are warm, friendly, extroverted people, who take a keen interest in their fellow-men. They at least try to base their business ethics on the Golden Rule and genuinely like to feel that they are in business not merely to make money, but to render a service to the community.

American etiquette is based on British etiquette, so that, generally speaking, if you just carry on as usual you will be doing the right thing. What will make you seem a little different, however, is the fact that many Americans do not follow the rules, but have a breezy, informal way of their own.

This is why countless Americans say 'Hallo' when introduced and cut up all their meat at one 'go', then eat it with a fork in their right hand.

Businessmen are slightly more formal or more 'correct', as they say in Europe, and you will find almost all American businessmen shake hands and say 'How do you do?', as if to the manner born. With introductions, the rules are exactly the same as in Britain, even down to the lady choosing whether or not to shake hands. So the form for you should be 'carry on as usual, but do not be surprised at the many deviations you will come across, especially when you move away from the strictly business circle.'

Americans do not stand on ceremony and before long you will certainly be on first-name terms with most of your business connections. It is a sign of friendliness, not rudeness, to use people's first name and even older women employees resent being called Mrs Smith, feeling that you consider them 'older', rather than one of the girls. All American women like to be considered girls, whether eight or eighty.

It is most important that you understand the American habit of asking lots of personal questions immediately upon acquaintance. What they are doing is showing interest in you, not prying. The fact is that Americans *are* interested in others and if you are honest with yourself you will admit that the Briton's habit of 'minding his own business' and not asking personal questions stems not so much from good manners as from natural caution or in some cases sheer indifference. Do not therefore wax red and angry when your new American acquaintance inquires about your home, your family, your hobbies and so on. Just relax, answer his questions, and thank God that someone cares so much about you.

Americans do a tremendous lot of business entertaining in the home and American wives enter very much into the spirit of the thing and attempt to help their husbands by being gracious hostesses. Most at-home entertaining is very informal, but there *are* American families where all the formalities are observed. At formal dinners, the same rules apply as in Britain, including seating arrangements, taking the ladies in to dinner and so on. If ashtrays are already on the table, you may begin to smoke after the main course. Otherwise, the hostess has them handed around after the salad. In some households the gentlemen escort the ladies to the drawing-room, upon a signal from the hostess, then leave them there and retire to the smoking-room for about twenty minutes or so. In other cases, the ladies leave on their own, as in England, and the men stay behind for their coffee and liqueurs. This, of course, only happens in very 'upper crust' circles.

When writing to Americans you will be anxious to follow

the correct forms. Americans do not commit the error of putting 'Messrs' before a company name. In fact, they never use it at all. They begin their letters 'Gentlemen' and end 'Yours truly'. If they begin 'Dear Mr Jones', then they end either with 'Yours sincerely', as we do in Britain, or 'Cordially yours'. 'Esq.', is, of course, a strictly British invention, although some American law firms and a handful of other organizations use it. The generally accepted American practice is simply 'Mr'. As for important personages or people with special titles or ranks, they are addressed as follows:

THE PRESIDENT
    Address on envelope The President
                       The White House
                       Washington, D.C.
    Letter opening Sir, (less formally: My Dear Mr President,)
    Salutation I have the honour to remain, most respectfully yours, (less formally: Very respectfully yours,)
    Verbally Mr President or Sir

THE VICE-PRESIDENT
    Address on envelope The Vice-President
                       United States Senate
                       Washington, D.C.
    Letter opening Sir, (less formally: My dear Mr Vice-President,)
    Salutation Very truly yours, (less formally: Sincerely yours,)
    Verbally Mr Vice-President or Sir

UNITED STATES SENATOR
    Address on envelope The Honorable
                       John Noble
                       United States Senate
                       Washington, D.C.
    Letter opening Sir, or Madam, (less formally: My dear Senator Noble,)
    Salutation Very truly yours, (less formally: Sincerely yours,)
    Verbally Senator, Senator Noble, or Sir or Madam

MEMBER OF THE UNITED STATES HOUSE OF REPRESENTATIVES
    Address on envelope The Honorable
                       Joseph W. Brown
                       United States House of Representatives
                       Washington, D.C.

Letter opening Sir, or Madam, (less formally: My dear Mr Brown,)
Salutation Very truly yours, (less formally: Sincerely yours,)
Verbally as for ordinary mortals

AMBASSADOR OF THE UNITED STATES
    Address on envelope The Honorable
                     Albert H. Smith
                     The Ambassador of the United States
                     American Embassy
                     Street address and city
    Letter opening Sir or Madam (less formally: My dear Mr Am·bassador or My dear Madam Ambassador,)
    Salutation Very truly yours, (less formally: Sincerely yours,)

GOVERNOR OF A STATE
    Address on envelope The Honorable
                     Alfred M. Mellor
                     Governor of Idaho
                     Boise, Idaho
    Letter opening Sir, (less formally: Dear Governor Mellor,)
    Salutation Very truly yours, (less formally: Sincerely yours,)

State Senators and Representatives are addressed in the same ways as u.s. Senators and Representatives, with the appropriate address. You will notice that, unlike the British custom, 'The Honorable' stands on its own on the first line. You will also have noted the American spelling.

MAYOR
    Address on envelope His (or Her) Honor the Mayor
                     City Hall
                     Easton, Maryland
    Letter opening Sir, (or Madam,) (less formally: Dear Mayor Wilkins,)
    Salutation Very truly yours, (less formally: Sincerely yours,)
    Verbally Mr Mayor or Madam Mayor

JUDGE
    Address on envelope The Honorable
                     Joseph Weeks
                     Justice, Appellate Division
                     Supreme Court of the State of New York
                     Albany, New York

Letter opening Sir, (less formally: Dear Judge Weeks,)
Salutation Very truly yours, (less formally: Sincerely yours,)
Verbally Mr Justice

AFRICA

It is quite possible to fly to Lagos, Accra, or any other large African city, put up at an air-conditioned hotel, meet your local agent – who will probably be an expatriate Englishman – discuss your business and then fly back without having had any contact whatsoever with Africa or Africans. Hundreds, if not thousands, of British businessmen do this every year and for them this section of the book is superfluous.

If, on the other hand, you are alive to the possibilities which the vast African Continent has to offer, if you appreciate the need to go there and meet the African on his home territory, rather than being pipped at the post by the more enterprising Americans, Japanese, and Germans, then you will want to discard completely the old colonial habits and look upon Africa as a new market to be tackled with an open mind and an open heart.

It is most important that you start out for Africa with the right attitude, that you realize an Englishman is no longer the Big White Chief visiting his Colonies, but simply a businessman hoping to sell his wares to his African counterpart. You will be quite mistaken if you believe that this African businessman is a savage in a business suit. On the contrary, in nine cases out of ten, he will be British-educated, will have a degree or even two from a British or American University, will have been called to the Bar or will have spent a few years teaching or in government. In many instances he will hold a Government post as well as running his own business. In other words, the African businessman belongs to the top social and cultural class in his country and will often be not merely the equal of the visiting British businessman, but his superior in intelligence, education, and social status.

It is almost essential that you spend some time acquiring at least a rudimentary background knowledge of the countries you plan to visit. If you have time to read only one book, then it should be *Africa: A Market Profile* by Dr T. L. V. Blair.* In it you will find suggested many other books which you could profitably read, including many by African authors. In addition, you should certainly read the appropriate booklets put out by the Board of Trade. They publish one for just about every country. They are called *Hints to Businessmen Visiting Sierra Leone*, or wherever.

There are also residential colleges all over the British Isles which offer courses for people about to leave for far-away places, including Africa. Farnham Castle in Surrey is one such college. There you can take a short residential course, lasting from Monday to Friday, on the various parts of Africa, as well as India, Latin America, the West Indies, and the Middle East.

Thus armed with background knowledge and the right attitude, you will be in a far better position to make a successful trip, to win new friends and new customers. The rest is easy, for you will find that in former British territories the actual rules of etiquette are exactly the same as they are in England, since the African ruling classes were educated by the British. In former French territories you will find French customs and etiquette followed. In fact, you will find that Africans have taken on the protective colouring of the Colonial power formerly ruling, with the former British contingent affecting a reserved, formal exterior and the French contingent a Latin dash and *galanterie*.

Hours of business are apt to vary somewhat from country to country, and so does the custom in clothing. In Liberia, for instance, clothing is rather more formal than might be expected in a tropical country. White drill suits are hardly ever worn, and tropical-weight lounge suits with collar and tie are the order of the day. On the other hand, in the Upper Volta, tropical trousers and an open-neck shirt are usually worn for normal business calls, although a jacket with collar and tie is *de rigueur* for official calls. All of these details are given in the Board of Trade booklets already mentioned and you should arm yourself with one for every country you intend to visit.

Business entertaining usually takes place in hotels and this applies both ways. In some countries, such as Nigeria and Ghana, a great deal of lively social life goes on, including cocktail parties,

* Business Publications Limited, 1965, 45s.

supper parties, and dancing, to which the visiting businessman is frequently invited.

Some parts of Africa are, of course, Muslim, and in the next section you will find hints on behaviour in Muslim countries.

An excellent maxim when travelling in Africa on business is to stick to your business and refrain from criticizing or commenting upon local customs, the Government, the heads of state, primitive conditions or anything else of a delicate nature. All young countries are extremely sensitive to criticism and this applies not only to Africa, but to Latin America and the U.S.A. of yesteryear. It is perfectly natural that this should be so and it does not behove us to scoff. In any event, friends and customers are not won by criticizing or being supercilious.

Africans will not admire you for 'going native' any more than for being 'high hat'. The answer, in fact, is just to be yourself and, if possible, a warmer and more sympathetic self. Not only your hosts, but you yourself will be the better for it.

ISLAM

Quite a substantial percentage of the African population is Muslim. This includes 44 per cent of Nigeria and most of the Sudan and Mali, not to mention Egypt and the other Arab countries in North Africa. In addition, there are, of course, the Muslim countries in the Middle East, as well as Turkey and Pakistan.

The interesting thing about Islam is that it is more than a religion, it is a complete way of life. It is true that some Muslim countries follow more closely in the footsteps of the Prophet than others. It is also true that there are several sects in Islam. In spite of this, Islam is far more interwoven with the everyday life of the people than is Christianity and it follows that the courteous visitor from abroad will be careful not to cause offence by his ignorance of Islamic customs and taboos.

The Islamic day of rest is Friday and you should, therefore, expect to find Government offices closed on a Friday in certain countries, including Iran, Libya, and Egypt. It is not however unlawful to work on a Friday and most businesses in Muslim countries are open as in other countries, with office hours which vary from country to country and frequently from season to season.

Muslims do not eat pork, neither do they drink alcoholic beverages. It is therefore in bad taste for a non-Muslim host to offer such foods to his Muslim guests. Some countries, such as Libya, are very observant of this rule, while others are considerably less so. It is up to you to use tact and delicacy in this matter.

Ramadan is the fasting month. During this time all able-bodied Muslims over fourteen are required to refrain from eating, drinking, and smoking from dawn to sunset. It follows that it would be extremely discourteous to give a luncheon party for Muslim guests during Ramadan. Neither should you yourself break the fast or smoke in public during the daytime, except, of course, in your hotel or in restaurants catering for Europeans. During this month, a dinner-party, timed at sunset, would be both correct and very acceptable.

In some Muslim countries, particularly Pakistan, Iran, and Iraq, it is not in good taste to give parties during Muharram, the first month of the Islamic year. This is because Husain, the grandson of the Prophet, was murdered on the tenth day of this month.

It is not possible to equate exactly the Islamic calendar with our own, because the months vary from year to year, coming approximately eleven days earlier every year. At the moment, Ramadan falls from about mid-December to about mid-January. Some countries make a holiday of the first day of Ramadan, in Libya the first three days of Ramadan are holidays, while other countries have a holiday on the last day. Otherwise, it is business as usual during this holy month.

If you are with your family, it is perfectly in order to invite your Muslim friends with their wives but, generally speaking, women are segregated and keep entirely out of the picture. You do not ask after a man's wife, but after his 'House'. Otherwise, it is safest to leave the womenfolk entirely alone. So many taboos surround them that it is all too easy to make a bad mistake.

If invited to a traditional Arab meal consisting of numerous courses, bear in mind that food is eaten with the fingers of the right hand, using thumb, index finger, and middle finger only. While a guest is expected to partake of some of each course, it is perfectly in order to eat frugally. On no account should you turn down the piece of barbecued lamb which your host will offer you and you should likewise accept all three cups of mint tea which your Moroccan host will offer you after your meal. Food should neither be offered nor accepted with the left hand.

'It is not done to point to someone with the sole of your foot'

It is not done to point at someone with the sole of your foot. One can hardly imagine an Englishman attempting such a feat, but it can happen accidentally if you cross your legs. The moral, therefore, is keep both feet on the ground.

Theoretically, Christians are welcome at the Mosque any time they wish. Tradition has it, in fact, that a Christian delegation stayed at the Mosque at Medina as guests of the Prophet and that they even performed their religious ceremonies there, with his full knowledge and approval. In practice, however, you would do well to ask each time, for there are some Mosques which are definitely not open to strangers.

OTHER LANDS

How to behave in other countries is simple enough. Follow British procedure in Australia and in former British colonies; British procedure with a dash of American relaxation in Canada; be very careful of treading on delicate nationalistic corns in the newly-independent countries, wherever they may be.

In Latin America, remember that you are dealing with Latins, in spite of the strong admixture of British and German blood. The Argentines are extremely formal in their dress and wear a collar and tie even for a river trip through the jungle. They are very nationalistic and it is diplomatic to praise everything praiseworthy and to criticize nothing.

Greetings between men are apt to be very effusive, and prolonged mutual back-slapping is the order of the day. Women call for very much more conservative treatment, since many of the old Spanish customs still linger on.

The gayest, most informal, and perhaps least Latin of the South Americans are the Brazilians. They are full of fun and will cheerfully laugh at you if you attempt a few words of Portuguese and come a cropper, something a Spaniard would never do. If your Brazilian agent moves towards you with outstretched arms, then clasps you in a mighty bear-hug and begins pounding your back with both his hands you will know you are experiencing an *abraço a brasileira* – quite a traumatic experience for an innocent Briton!

In all these countries courtesy, thoughtfulness, and empathy are really all you need to get by with flying colours. Follow the Golden Rule and you cannot go wrong.

JAPAN

There is one country, however, where no amount of thoughtfulness and consideration for others will help; where empathy is impossible and where your antennae will persistently send you the wrong signals. This country is Japan. The reason for this is that Japanese standards and philosophies are and have been entirely different from ours for several thousand years.

The Japanese is a product of a unique civilization. It might be said that for him a certain behaviour is laid down for every event of his private and public life. This behaviour is based on his obligations – to himself, to his fellow-men, to his country, and to the world – to his position, sex, age, and family ties. His society was built on a class and rank system in which position, manners, and 'face' were the supreme values.

This means that:

1 A Japanese businessman will view his relationship with his employees or with a client company in the light of their personal obligation to him or of his obligation to them. An objective, business-like approach would be quite alien to him.

2 Manners – the outward form – are the ultimate virtue. There is a Japanese way of doing everything and since conformity used to be enforced in the most brutal and cruel way, it has become part of the Japanese make-up and very hard to shed.

3 Saving face or helping the other fellow to save face is an occupation which employs a great deal of Japanese time.

When making your first business trip to Japan, you should allow three to four weeks. You would be wise to consider it an exploratory trip, because that is all you can expect to do in Japan in that length of time. Neither should you expect any concrete results in three to four months – fourteen months would probably be nearer the mark. Everything takes three times as long in Japan as it does in Europe and this very much includes business.

Travel by Japan Airlines and stay in first-class hotels to show 'face'. If a Japanese business friend is meeting you, let him see you coming out of the first class, not 'economy'. This, once again, will give you 'face'.

Make sure you have plenty of trinkets with you, inexpensive little souvenirs to give away wherever you go. Also take your full quota of whisky, as it has become a status symbol in Japan and makes a very impressive special gift. Dunhill lighters also come under this heading. Have cards in English on one side and Japanese on the back. You can get them done within 24 hours in Japan.

Invite a businessman to your hotel, rather than suggesting you visit his office. If you invite one man, expect three or four of his colleagues to come with him. Don't expect them to be on time, however, but up to an hour late.

On no account should you talk business on this first contact. This is the height of bad manners in Japan. Talk about the weather, your trip, Japan, golf – especially golf. This is a favourite sport with Japanese businessmen and many a large contract is made on the golf-course.

Speak slowly and distinctly, without raising your voice, and keep as nearly as you can to basic English. Do not ask your Japanese guest whether he understands, because that leaves him no choice but to say 'Yes', 'Yes' with that mysterious Japanese smile. He would lose face if he admitted he did not understand.

The social side is extremely important in Japan and you should be prepared to be invited to dinner parties in geisha houses lasting from two to three hours. Do bear in mind that the geishas are there only to serve your meal and to entertain you with conversation, music, and singing. You would certainly blot your copybook very badly if you assumed they had any other function or if you failed to behave in a gentlemanly way towards them. Meanwhile, your Japanese hosts will be very quickly getting the worse for drink and you will have little difficulty in showing 'face' by remaining stone-cold sober after several tiny cups of saki.

The best way you can reciprocate this hospitality which, incidentally, will have cost your Japanese host the earth, is a luncheon party in your hotel.

At luncheon parties, at the geisha house, on the golf-course – this is where business is transacted in the leisurely Japanese way. Pressure tactics are extremely distasteful to the Japanese and so indeed is the direct Western way of putting one's cards on the table and calling a spade a spade.

Nowhere more than in Japan, therefore, will you find La Fontaine's advice about patience and time more useful. Likewise, previous preparation will be doubly useful when dealing with the

Japanese. The Japanese civilization is so complex, so startling, and so unusual that you cannot hope even to begin to understand it unless you make a serious attempt to do so. A book which has steered countless American businessmen in the right direction since its publication is *Japanese Manners and Ethics in Business* by Boye De Mente,* but it may be difficult to get hold of a copy in Britain. A more recent book which gives a great deal of useful background information is *A Businessman's Japan* by Takeshi Sato.† Introductory courses on Japan are available at various colleges across the country, as mentioned for Africa, and there is also a company which specializes in advising businessmen who are anxious to break into the Japanese market or are about to make their first business trip there. This is the Anglo-Japanese Industrial Service of 15 New Burlington Street, London, W.1.

* East Asia Publishing Company Limited, 1961.
† Michael Joseph Limited, 1964.

N

appendix one

surnames with tricky pronunciations

The right way to pronounce a person's surname is the way he or she likes it pronounced. This is one more reason for listening carefully when you are introduced to anyone, since all of us are rather sensitive to the way our names are spelt and pronounced. Here is a short list of surnames which are not usually pronounced as written. Their usual pronunciation is given alongside, but do bear in mind that there *are* people with these surnames who pronounce them exactly as written, probably because they have come across so many people who did not know the correct form and finally gave up the struggle:

spelling	pronunciation	spelling	pronunciation
Beauchamp	Beecham	Bouchier	Bowcher
Beauclerk	Boclare		(Some people
Beaulieu	Bewly		with this sur-
Belvoir	Beaver		name pronounce
Berkeley	Barkly		it Booshay)
Bertie	Barty	Brough	Bruff
Bicester	Bister	Brougham	Broom
Blount	Blunt	Buccleuch	Bucklew

spelling	pronunciation	spelling	pronunciation
Buchan	Buckan	Keighley	Keethly
Burleigh	Burly	Kerr	Car
Cadogan	Caduggan	Knollys	Noles
Cecil	Sissil	Lefevre	Lefever
Cholmondeley	Chumly	Lemaistre	Lemayter
Clough	Cluff	Leveson-Gower	Loosen-Gore
Cockbain	Cobàin	Mackay	Mc-eye
Cockburn	Coburn	McLeod	McCloud
Colquhoun	Cohòon	Mainwaring	Mannering
Conesford	Connisford	Marjoribanks	Marchbanks
Conyngham	Cunningham	Menzies	Minges (but not
Cowper	Cooper		always)
Crichton	Cryton		(hard 'g')
Derby	Darby	Meux	Mews or Mewks
Devereux	Deveroo	Millet	Millay
Donoughmore	Donomore	Molyneux	Moliner or
Drogheda	Droider		Molinewks
Duchesne	Dukain	Montgomery	Mungùmery
Dumaresq	Dumèrrick	Pepys	Peeps (but not
Elgin	Elguin		always)
Eyre	Air	Petre	Peter
Farquhar	Farkwar	Ponsonby	Punsunby
Farquharson	Farkerson	Raleigh	Rawly
Faulk	Foke	Ruthven	Rivn
Geoghegan	Gagan	St John	Sinjun
Gifford	Jifford	St Leger	Sellinjer
Glamis	Glahms	Sandys	Sands
Gough	Goff	Strachan	Strawn
Hardinge	Harding	Tollemache	Tolmash
Harewood	Harwood	Tyrwhitt	Tirritt
Hawarden	Haywarden	Vaughan	Vawn
Heathcote	Hethcut	Villiers	Villers
Hertford	Harford	Waldegrave	Walgrave
Home	Hume (but not always)	Wemyss	Weems

appendix two

foreign expressions
in use in Britain

In Victorian times, it was the vogue to pepper one's speech with
French phrases and Queen Victoria's letters are full of them. But
this vogue has long passed and it is now considered pretentious
to use foreign expressions without just cause. However, you
would be ill-advised automatically to label a person as pretentious
because he has a habit of interlarding his speech with foreign
expressions. When a person is a linguist and has lived abroad for
a number of years, he sometimes has an irresistible urge to use
one of the many foreign expressions he knows, if it happens to
convey the exact shade of meaning he has in mind. People with
a love of language are quite apt to do this and it should not be
considered a mortal sin.

To use a foreign word merely to show off is, of course, different
again, and not to be recommended. Here are some of the foreign
expressions used in Britain with some frequency, together with
their approximate pronunciation and meaning. Some such words
have almost been adopted into the English language and are
pronounced in an anglicized way. These are marked 'English
pron.' Many people in Britain pronounce the remaining words
also with a very British accent, but it does seem more logical to

speak either English or French, rather than to make an unhappy amalgam of the two:

expression*	pronunciation	meaning
accouchement (F)	ahkooshman	confinement
à deux (F)	ah der	together (of two people)
ad infinitum (L)	ad infinytum	to infinity, i.e. for ever
affaire de cœur (F)	ahfer de ker	affair of the heart, i.e. romance
aide-de-camp (F)	ade de com	officer assisting general
al fresco (I)	ahl fresco	in the open air
alter ego (L)	alter ego	other self
anno Domini (L)	anno Dominee	in the year of the Lord
aplomb (F)	ahplon	self-possession
au fait (F)	o feh	acquainted with, in the know
au revoir (F)	o revwar	until we meet again
beau monde (F)	bo maunde	the fashionable world
bel canto (I)	bel cahnto	singing characterized by a full, rich, broad tone and fine technique
belles-lettres (F)	bell letr	writings or studies of purely literary kind
bête noire (F)	bet nwahr	pet aversion
billet-doux (F)	bilidoo (English pron.)	love-letter, used mostly jocularly in Britain
bonne bouche (F)	bonn boosh	tasty morsel
carte blanche (F)	cart blansh	free hand
cause célèbre (F)	cause selebr	lawsuit that excites much attention
caveat emptor (L)	cahvehaht emptor	let the buyer beware
chacun à son goût (F)	shakun ah son goo	everyone to his taste
chignon (F)	sheegnon	a bun (hair style)
coiffure (F)	kwafur	hair style
comme il faut (F)	com eel foh	decorous, proper
compos mentis (L)	composs mentiss	of sound mind
contretemps (F)	contr tahn	hitch, setback
corps de ballet (F)	cor de balley	company of ballet dancers
coup de grâce (F)	coo de grass	final stroke
coup d'état (F)	coo d'ehtah	violent or illegal change of government
cri de cœur (F)	cree de ker	passionate appeal, complaint or protest

* Each expression is marked either F, I, L, or G, according to whether French, Italian, Latin, or German.

expression*	pronunciation	meaning
debut (F)	debu (English pron.)	first appearance in society, on stage, etc.
Deo volente (L)	deho volenteh	God willing
distingué (F)	distangeh	distinguished, elegant
double entendre (F)	dooble entahndr	double meaning
en deshabillé (F)	on desabeeyay	in a state of undress
en famille (F)	on famee	with one's family, i.e. at home
en passant (F)	on passon	in passing, by the way
entre-nous (F)	ontre noo	between ourselves
et alia (L)	et alia	and others
ex-officio (L)	ex-oficio	arising out of his office
fait accompli (F)	fett accomplee	accomplished fact
faux-pas (F)	foh pah	an offence against social convention, or a compromising act
fin-de-siècle (F)	fan de see eckle	characteristic of the end of the ninteenth century, decadent
hors de combat (F)	orr de combah	out of the fight, disabled
hors d'œuvre (F)	or dervre	first course
idem (L)	eedem	the same
infra dig. (L) (abbr. for infra dignitatem)	infra dig (hard 'g')	beneath one's dignity
ingénue (F)	onjehnoo	innocent girl, actress playing such a part
insouciance (F)	onsoosions	unconcern
inter alia (L)	inter alia	among other things
ipso facto (L)	ipso facto	by the very fact
laisser-aller (F)	lehsseh ahlleh	unconstrained freedom
laisser-faire (F)	lehsseh fer	Government abstention from interference, especially in commerce
lapsus mentis (L)	lahpsus mentis	lapse of memory
Lebensraum (G)	Lehbensrahoom	room to live and develop
locum tenens (L)	locum tenens	deputy (a doctor's stand-in is called a locum)
manqué (F)	mahnkeh	(after noun) unsuccessful
marriage de convenance (F)	mahriahj de conv-nahns	marriage of convenience
marron glacé (F)	mahrron glahseh	candied chestnuts
mêlée (F)	m'leh	skirmish

* Each expression is marked either F, I, L, or G, according to whether French, Italian, Latin, or German.

expression*	pronunciation	meaning
métier (F)	mehtieh	one's trade
mot juste (F)	moh just	word that conveys just the right shade of meaning
noblesse oblige (F)	nobless obleej	rank imposes obligations
nom-de-guerre (F)	nom de guer	pseudonym
nom-de-plume (F)	nom de plume	author's pseudonym
non sequitur (L)	non sequiter	an illogical inference
nouveau riche (F)	noovoh rish	wealthy upstart
omnia vincit amor (L)	omniah vinsit amor	love conquers all
par excellence (F)	par excelans	above all, pre-eminently
parvenu (F)	parvenoo	upstart
pas-de-deux (F)	pah de der	dance for two (ballet)
passé (F)	passeh	outmoded
penchant (F)	panshahn	inclination, liking for
per ardua ad astra (L)	per arduah ad astra	through hardship to the stars (Motto of the Royal Air Force)
per capita (L)	per capitah	per head
pied à terre (F)	pee-ehdahtare	temporary lodging
poseur (F)	poser	a show-off
poste restante (F)	post restahnt	a department in the post office where letters are kept until called for
prima facie (L)	preemah fachie	on the face of it, at first sight
raconteur (F)	raconter	story-teller, conversationalist
raconteuse (F)	raconterse	story-teller
raison d'être (F)	rehson detre	reason for being
rapprochement (F)	rapproshmon	reconciliation, drawing together
répondez s'il vous plaît (F)	rehpondeh sil voo play	please reply (see Chapter 9)
requiescat in pace (L)	rekwee-eskat in pahcheh	may he rest in peace
robe-de-chambre (F)	robe de shambr	dressing gown
savoir-faire (F)	savwar fair	skill, tact, dexterity
savoir vivre (F)	savwar vivr	polished manners
soupçon (F)	soopson	dash of, very small quantity (literally, suspicion)
stet (L)	stet	let it stand
sub-judice (L)	sub joodissay	under adjudication

* Each expression is marked either F, I, L, or G, according to whether French, Italian, Latin, or German.

expression*	pronunciation	meaning
sub-rosa (L)	sub rosah	privately, secretly
succès d'estime (F)	suxeh desteem	respectful but cool reception given to a performance
succès fou (F)	suxeh foo	a great success
tempus fugit (L)	tempus foojit	time flies
tête-à-tête (F)	tetahtet	private interview or conversation
tour de force (F)	tour de force	feat of strength
vide (L)	veedie	see (as in *vide supra*, see above, *vide infra*, see below, etc.)
vingt-et-un (F)	vant eh un	twenty-one, a card game
voilà (F)	vwalah	there!

* Each expression is marked either F, I, L, or G, according to whether French, Italian, Latin, or German.

Index